Don't Dare Die
A Copy

Life Skills Book For Teens:
Everything Your Parents Never Told
You.

Kay Love

Copyright

Contents

About The Author

K ay Love is a mother of an adult son and a childcare provider for 20 years. She has prepared children for school where they have gone into gifted and talented programs with the help of involved parents. During this time, a lack of support from city and childcare networks was apparent. There were more work that needed to be done.

Over the years, children haven't been prepared with the skills to get through life. Parents either didn't correct the wrong or thought everything a child did was appealing. Whether you agree with me or not, children have been lost or forgotten. For whatever reason, our children are being failed and we need to get them back on track and bring the life lessons that were lost. With that passion, I have decided to write this book to get teens ready for life and to help parents to learn some tools to prepare their teens. With that being said, let's drive in and walk this journey together. Thank you.

Acknowledgment

This book is dedicated to a woman who loved children and she called them her Little Jewels which are her precious gems. She dedicated 40 years to teaching and raising children in her care and she was my mentor.
Marva Hawkins Williams Waithe
May 27, 1944-October 31, 2020

Introduction

You're a high school student. You've just gotten your first part-time job at a local fast-food restaurant. On your first day, you're nervous and excited—but slightly overwhelmed by all the new responsibilities and expectations.

As you nervously serve customers on your first day, you suddenly hear a group of your friends laughing and joking in the corner. You approach them, hoping for some friendly support, but they start teasing you for working in a fast-food restaurant. They tell you that you're wasting your time. You feel embarrassed and frustrated.

You start questioning yourself for working there—wanting to make all their awful words disappear. However, before you do, consider what's truly important. Is it more important to impress your friends, learn valuable skills, and earn a paycheck? Are you willing to relinquish your goals just to fit in with the crowd?

This moment is something that many teens can relate to, whether they're starting a new job, taking on new responsibilities at school or home, or just trying to navigate the ups and downs of teenage life.

There's no denying that life as a teenager can be overwhelming. You're dealing with the inevitable awkwardness of growing up. It can feel like you're stumbling around in the dark, unsure of where you belong.

On the one hand, you feel like a child, but on the other hand, you're expected to act like an adult. You have new responsibilities to juggle. You honestly don't know where you stand. But fear not; you're not alone.

As a high school student, it's crucial to start developing essential life skills that will prepare you for the future. You will learn how to master the often subtle art of communication. You will also learn how to avoid falling prey to peer pressure and form more meaningful relationships.

To help prepare you for your upcoming adult years, you will also learn the dangers of social media addiction and drug use. You will also learn to avoid risky behaviors and manage your finances confidently and easily.

Chapter 1: Parents and Teens Communication

Sophie was a typical 16-year-old high school student who loved hanging out with friends and scrolling through social media. She was going through many changes in her life, from dealing with school stress to navigating her first relationship. However, she often felt that her parents didn't understand her and couldn't communicate with them.

One day, Sophie's mom came into her room and asked, "Can we talk?" Sophie's heart sank, and she immediately started to feel anxious. She assumed that her mom would lecture her about her grades or something she did wrong. Despite feeling uneasy, Sophie agreed to have the conversation.

To her surprise, her mom started the conversation by asking her how she was doing and what was happening in her life. Sophie felt relieved that her mom was genuinely interested in her life and wasn't there to scold her. They discussed everything, from school and friends to relationships and plans. It was a conversation that Sophie longed to have with her mom.

After that day, Sophie realized that the phrase "Can we talk?" didn't have to evoke negative emotions. Instead, it could be an opportunity for an open and honest conversation with her parents. She started using this phrase herself, initiating conversations with her parents whenever she needed to talk.

Through these conversations, Sophie's relationship with her parents grew stronger. She learned to communicate her needs and feelings effectively, and her parents learned to listen without judgment. The phrase "Can we talk?" became a regular part of their communication, and they started to have more meaningful conversations than ever before.

Sophie learned that effective communication was essential in building a healthy relationship with her parents and that by using the phrase "Can we talk?" she could initiate conversations that strengthened their bond.

"Can we talk?" is a common phrase used to start a sensitive or difficult conversation, and it can evoke emotions from anxiety to hopefulness. While this phrase may make some people uncomfortable, it's important to remember that effective communication is critical in any relationship between parents and their children. Building trust, understanding, and respect through communication can help parents stay connected with their children's lives.

Communication between parents and teenagers is often challenging and can lead to misunderstandings and conflicts. To prevent this, both parties must be open and honest. Your parents must listen without judgment, while you must respectfully communicate your needs and desires.

Effective communication is even more crucial during your teen years when you experience many changes and challenges while transitioning into adulthood.

Parent-teen communication involves various aspects, such as improving listening skills, utilizing effective communication techniques, and learning to have difficult conversations. Additionally, nonverbal skills can also play a significant role in communication.

Why Is Communication Important?

It is unsurprising to realize that everything changes as you age. As you enter your teenage years, you become more aware of the world. You are no longer a child who can have adults speak for you.

As you approach adulthood, you start to form your own unique beliefs separate from your parents. You will further develop language and cognitive skills—essential for academic and personal growth.

In your quest to become an adult, you need to learn how to communicate effectively. But then that invokes the question of what exactly is 'effective communication?' Adrienne Duke and Jennifer Kerpelman, Associate Professor, and former Extension Specialist, respectively, define it as "occurring when the person sending a message makes it clear and easy to understand, and the person on the receiving end understands the message as the sender intended" (2021, para. 2).

Communication is necessary to foster relationships, improve social skills, and establish positive connections. Excellent communication skills enable you to articulate your thoughts and emotions, comprehend diverse viewpoints, and negotiate skillfully.

Creating positive relationships with parents, teachers, and peers can enhance your emotional and mental well-being by giving you a sense of belonging, support, and confidence. As you progress into adulthood, you will inevitably rely on a role model, whoever that may be, for guidance and advice. Effective communication with parents, teachers, and other adults can facilitate this process by offering valuable insights from their experiences. With this knowledge, you can make more informed decisions and avoid risky behaviors.

Effective communication with your parents, particularly when discussing sensitive topics, requires creating a safe and non-judgmental environment that fosters honesty, transparency, and respect for each other's opinions and beliefs. Building a stronger bond with your parents requires active listening and caring for each other's views. Active listening is "asking questions about the other person's feelings, reiterating the most important information" (Ivypanda, 2020, para. 6).

Listening also involves showing empathy and being supportive, even when you disagree. "In the process of active listening, there is no place for judgment because one family member emphatically tries to understand what the other person is feeling and thinking" (Ivypanda, 2020, para 6).

Just like with everything, it is essential to be flexible when communicating. "Flexibility comes when you can see a situation for what it is, rather than what you want it to be, and accept those circumstances" (Brown, 2018, para. 5).

Being flexible in your communication approach involves being open-minded and listening to all perspectives. "Adapting a flexible mindset means rolling with the punches and choosing not to let things affect you when they do not go as planned (Brown, 2018). When you let go of being rigid, you begin to look at life differently—which will trickle down in all aspects of your life. You will begin to see life more as a "series of opportunities to learn from" (Brown, 2018, para. 13) and start communicating better.

Nonverbal Communication

Reading and interpreting nonverbal cues will help you better understand others, enhancing your communication skills. But first, the question is, what is nonverbal communication?

Nonverbal communication, sometimes called body language, transmits information through body language, facial expressions, eye contact, tone of voice, gestures, et cetera. It often conveys emotions, attitudes, and intentions more effectively than words alone. After all, haven't you heard the phrase: "Actions speak louder than words."

While nonverbal cues can be intentional or unintentional, they will influence how people perceive and respond to verbal messages. Nonverbal communication will impact the success or failure of social interactions.

Unfortunately, observing others is the only way to hone your nonverbal skills. You must start paying attention to others' body language, facial expressions, and tone of voice during conversations.

You should start by paying attention to others' eyes. The eyes are a critical element of nonverbal communication, often called the "window to the soul." Eye contact, movements, and expressions provide valuable information about emotions and intentions. For instance, avoiding eye contact may imply shyness or discomfort, while prolonged eye contact can suggest interest or aggression.

Besides the eyes, facial expressions can reveal much about a person. Sometimes subtle movements of the mouth, nose, and eyebrows can reveal much about someone. A furrowed brow may indicate confusion or worry, while a smile can convey happiness or warmth.

Other nonverbal cues include gestures, body language, posture, and touch. Gestures such as hand movements and nods can provide insight into a person's feelings and thoughts. For example, a person with crossed arms may signal discomfort or defensiveness, while an open posture with uncrossed arms may signal openness or receptiveness. Different poses can also convey different confidence, authority, or insecurity levels.

Physical touch can convey warmth, support, and reassurance. A firm handshake may suggest respect or confidence, while a hug may convey affection and warmth. One can gain insight into others' emotional states and intentions by paying attention to physical touch.

You should be mindful of cultural differences in nonverbal communication. Different cultures may have different norms for body language, facial expressions, and physical touch. Awareness of and respecting these differences is essential when communicating with people from different backgrounds.

Chapter 2: Relationships

When Sarah was 16, she started dating Jack. Jack was charming, confident, and popular. Sarah was smitten with him and felt lucky to be his girlfriend.

However, over time, Sarah noticed red flags in their relationship. Jack would often belittle her in front of his friends and get jealous and controlling if she talked to other guys. Sarah started to feel like she was walking on eggshells around Jack, knowing something was wrong.

Despite the warning signs, Sarah stayed in the relationship, hoping things would improve. She did not want to be alone, and she did not want to admit that she had made a mistake.

It was not until Sarah's parents started to express concerns about her relationship that she realized something was seriously wrong. They had noticed changes in her behavior and demeanor and seen how Jack treated her.

Sarah's parents encouraged her to end the relationship and focus on building healthy relationships in the future. They talked to her about how unhealthy relationships can lead to a cycle of abuse and how it is essential to recognize red flags and know when to walk away.

Sarah took their advice and ended things. It was not easy, but it was the right decision. She took time to heal and focus on herself, and she learned valuable lessons about the importance of setting boundaries, recognizing red flags, and fostering healthy relationships.

Years later, Sarah looked back on that experience with gratitude. She realized that her parents' guidance had helped her avoid potentially devastating consequences and had set her on the path toward healthy, fulfilling relationships in the future.

As teenagers, relationships can be exciting and confusing all at once. So, while it's natural to want to explore romantic connections, you also should be mindful of potential red flags and know how to build healthy relationships.

The connections we form with our parents can impact our expectations and communication styles in future romantic connections, so developing healthy relationships with them is crucial.

Why Do Relationships Matter?

Humans are social creatures who crave connections as soon as we are born. Relationships shape our identity, emotional well-being, and psychological and physical health. Healthy relationships offer a sense of belonging, companionship, and purpose that promote growth and maturity in all areas of life.

Your early childhood experiences—particularly the bond formed with your parents or guardians—will impact your ability to form healthy relationships later in life. You will form relationships with friends, family, coworkers, and romantic partners crucial to your personal development.

Healthy relationships provide incredible emotional support, allowing loved ones to offer feedback on behavior and thoughts, challenge assumptions, and offer constructive criticism. Healthy relationships will also help you practice important communication, empathy, and compromise skills.

Having someone to confide in during difficult situations or challenges can reduce stress and anxiety. You should also prioritize emotional and physical well-being, which circles back to healthy relationships with those around you.

Potential Relationship Problems

Adolescence is a time of immense change; there is no doubt about that. As you age, many experiences will have the potential to disrupt and cause problems in the relationships you keep. These changes include starting college, moving to a new city or school, or changing family dynamics. These life transitions can strain all relationships, not just romantic ones.

As a teen, you may also face external pressures from school and family conflicts that will stress your relationships. As you mature, your interests, priorities, and values may shift, leading to conflicts within the relationship.

Another potential problem is when one person is unsure of their feelings. To avoid confusion or misunderstandings, you should communicate openly and honestly about your feelings and intentions to those you feel romantic feelings towards. Always be clear about what you want from your relationship. As Emani Brooks points out, "Pushing aside your feelings or your partner's feelings can lead to bigger problems in the future. That is why it is important always to be clear and direct, tell your partner what you think, need, and feel, and your partner should be able to do the same" (2022, para. 3). Be sure to pay attention to their actions and behavior, not words, to avoid misunderstandings.

Isolation can also cause various problems in teenage relationships. Isolation can be a lack of communication, understanding, or support within your relationship. It can also cause feelings of neglect and abandonment. After all, "most people in healthy relationships prioritize spending time together, though the amount of time you spend together can vary based on personal needs, work and other commitments, living arrangements, and so on" (Raypole, 2019, para. 23). Relationships of all kinds should enrich your life. They should "contribute to [your] sense of fulfillment, happiness, and connection. Your relationship may struggle if you feel more anxious, distressed, or unhappy around your partner" (Raypole, 2019, para. 37).

To avoid these problems, it is crucial to engage in the relationship, and prioritizing it is crucial. Spending quality time together, participating in shared activities, and engaging in meaningful conversations can help maintain a healthy and fulfilling connection.

Recognizing that not all relationships are healthy is crucial. Be aware of potential red flags and seek help when necessary. Trusted adults can help during this time, and you can seek the help of a therapist or counselor to find solutions that work for you. When partners are willing to listen to each other, be flexible, and work together, they can overcome these challenges and strengthen their relationship.

Red Flags in Relationships

Any relationship can have red flags. It is unfortunate but part of life. You may think of them only for romantic relationships, but that is untrue. Sometimes friendships—or even familial relationships—can have red flags present. These red flags indicate potential issues that may arise in the relationship and, if not addressed, can escalate into serious problems.

Mental and physical abuse is the most severe of the red flags. If one person is verbally or physically abusive towards the other, it is a sign of an unhealthy—and potentially dangerous relationship. "Many abusers will test their partners' boundaries by threatening to physically harm them to see if they can get away with doing so. It is never okay for your partner to call you names or physically hurt you. Abuse is something no one should ever have to deal with, no matter the form of abuse" (Brooks, 2022, para. 10). If you think you, or anyone you know, are part of any abusive relationship, you need to seek help immediately.

One red flag to look out for is the inability to be open with feelings. If one partner is reluctant to share their thoughts or emotions, it can create a communication barrier. This barrier can lead to misunderstandings and assumptions, which can cause conflict and, if left unaddressed, will lead to resentment.

Another red flag to watch out for is feeling pressured within the relationship. If one partner presses the other to do something they are uncomfortable with, it can create discomfort and anxiety. For instance, if one partner constantly pressures the other to have sex, this can create an unhealthy dynamic in the relationship. As Emani Brooks reminds us, "In a healthy relationship," no one "should ever force you to do anything that you do not agree or feel comfortable with" (2022, para. 5).

Jealousy is another typical red flag. If one partner is overly jealous or possessive, it can create feelings of insecurity and resentment.

Jealousy can also lead to controlling behavior, which can escalate into more severe issues. If one partner tries to control the other's actions, thoughts, or behaviors, it creates a power imbalance. Unaddressed power imbalances can quickly lead to emotional or physical abuse. After all, "there should be a healthy balance in the quality time you spend with each person in your life. If your partner gets angry when you spend time with someone other than them, that is an immediate red flag. You should never let someone take you away from others who are a part of your life and whom you love" (Brooks, 2022, para. 8).

Although abuse is usually considered more of an adult relationship problem, abuse can happen at any age. "Some teens have anger issues, and in most cases, people experience abuse for the first time by their significant other before the age of 24" (Brooks, 2022, para. 10), so it is good to be aware of all the warning signs.

Negative relationships can lead to emotional dysregulation, mental health problems like depression and anxiety, and unhealthy coping mechanisms like substance abuse or self-harm.

Healthy Adolescent Relationships

You must take the time to develop strong social relationships, including romantic relationships and friendships. The Office of Population Affairs says, "Adolescents often try on different identities and roles, and all of these relationships contribute to their identity formation" (2022, para. 1), meaning that these relationships will help you as you journey into adulthood.

Our relationships help us to "pursue dreams much bigger than ourselves and help to give us "greater curiosity, courage, strength, and wisdom" as "we venture into the unknown to become who we are meant to be" (Kim, 2021, para. 30). Healthy, loving relationships also help us to "recharge" from the stresses of our daily lives (Kim, 2021, para. 24).

A romantic partnership can "be an important way to develop social skills, learn about others, and grow emotionally. These relationships can also support adolescents' ability to develop positive relationships in other areas, including: in school, with employers, and with partners during adulthood" (Office of Population Affairs, 2022, para. 3). However, it is essential to recognize that an unhealthy relationship can cause stress and emotional turmoil. Therefore, while not essential for every teenager, a romantic partnership can be a valuable learning experience.

For those experiencing it for the first time, navigating a romantic relationship can be challenging. Unlike other relationships, a romantic one involves deeper emotional and physical intimacy and requires more effort and attention. However, it is possible to successfully navigate a romantic relationship with the right mindset and skills.

One of the most significant challenges of a romantic relationship is learning how to have one in the first place. It may be unfamiliar as a new type of relationship, particularly for those without prior experience. Building a healthy romantic relationship requires open communication, mutual respect, and trust.

Communication is vital when building a healthy romantic relationship. You must be open and honest with your partner to build and maintain a strong connection. Talking with your partner should feel good. After all, "you should be comfortable talking about any issues that come up, from things that happen in everyday life to more serious issues, such as mental health symptoms or financial concerns" (Raypole, 2019, para. 11).

You should feel completely safe sharing thoughts, feelings, and needs and actively listening when your partner shares theirs. "Partners in healthy relationships typically talk about the things going on in their lives: successes, failures, and everything in between" (Raypole, 2019, para. 10). You must also compromise and work through differences. After all, "Miscommunications can happen... But if you talk through an issue and they seem receptive but do not make any changes or seem to have completely forgotten what you talked about by the next day, that is also a warning sign" (Raypole, 2019, para. 55).

Another essential element of a healthy romantic relationship is mutual respect and trust. Respecting your partner's boundaries, opinions, and choices and receiving the same treatment in return is crucial. This means "You should always be able to speak your mind, and you both should allow each other to be a safe space where you can talk without any anger starting to form" (Brooks, 2020, para. 12). Genuine trust takes time and effort but is essential for the relationship's longevity. It is important to be vulnerable with your partner and trust that they will not judge you or betray your confidence.

As a teen, you are experiencing significant social and emotional growth, learning to navigate new social situations. The Office of Population Affairs suggests that "positive friendships provide youth companionship, support, and a sense of belonging. They can encourage or reinforce healthy behavior, like positive academic engagement; help youth develop positive social skills like cooperation, communication, conflict resolution, and resisting negative peer pressure; evidence suggests that positive friendships in adolescence can lay the groundwork for successful adult relationships, including romantic relationships" (2022, para. 6).

Positive friendships can encourage you to make healthy choices and avoid risky behaviors. Friendships can also offer opportunities for fun, relaxation, and developing new skills and interests. However, not all friendships are healthy. Parents and caregivers can help guide you toward positive friendships by monitoring social activities.

Relationship With Parents

Your relationship with your parents or caretakers is one of the most important relationships you will ever experience. The relationship has had the most effect on shaping you into the person you are today and, perhaps, even the person you will be as an adult.

There is no denying that your relationship has changed. You are not a child anymore. Sometimes, parents can react poorly to that change. Kevyn Gohu of Modern Parenting writes, "[parents] first start by denying it happens. [Parents] sometimes get so scandalized by the thought of our teens drinking beer that we forget we probably did that too at their age...It will take some time, but we eventually need to accept that they are not small anymore. As teens, they can exercise their ability to make decisions" (2021, para. 4).

You and your parents must communicate effectively to maintain a healthy parent-teen relationship. Your parents need to treat you like the teenager you now are, and not the child they remember you being. According to Fuligini and Eccles, as children transition into adolescence, it becomes necessary for their relationships to adapt and transform in order to accommodate their changing developmental requirements (1993). Fuligni and Eccles further note that the way families navigate this transitional period is likely to have significant consequences for the roles that parents and peers play in the developmental journey of adolescents (1993). If the transition is handled poorly, teens will move to put more and more value in their peers rather than what the parents have to say.

Your parents should create a supportive environment where you feel safe expressing your thoughts and emotions. It can be daunting to talk to your parents about sensitive situations. Still, open and honest communication can only thrive where you feel comfortable expressing yourself. Your parents must also respect your opinions and beliefs and foster an environment that allows for candid dialogue.

It is imperative to actively listen to what your parents are telling you. However, communication is a two-way street, so your parents must also pay attention to what you are saying, acknowledge your emotions, and respond appropriately. Fostering a stronger bond with your parents requires active listening and respect for each other's opinions. Active listening is "Asking questions about the other person's feelings, reiterating the most important information, as well as showing appreciation for an individual who tried to share his or her feelings with a family member" (Ivypanda, 2020, para. 6).

Listening also involves showing empathy and being supportive, even when you disagree. "Listening can be considered one of the most important aspects of successful communication within a family since it is crucial for understanding and being understood by other family members. There is no place for judgment because one member of a family emphatically tries to understand what the other person is feeling and thinking" (Ivypanda, 2020, para 6). After all, listening is critical. Duke and Kerpelman say it is the best way for parents to improve the parent-teen relationship. You want to feel "as if you matter" and by listening to your parents show you their support (2021, para 2 3).

Your parents should also respect your privacy, boundaries, and independence while setting appropriate boundaries for your safety and well-being. Your parents will show you they trust and respect you by recognizing and valuing your unique personality, interests, and strengths. Your parents should be consistent, reliable, and honest with you. They should be transparent with their expectations, rules, and consequences.

Spending quality time together and sharing positive experiences can help strengthen the bond between parent and teen. Activities or hobbies that you all enjoy, meaningful conversations, or simply enjoying each other's company can create lasting memories and help maintain a strong relationship.

Effects on Future Relationships

How your parents treated you throughout life has shaped your understanding of love, trust, and intimacy. Your parents have defined "some of your character's most important basic building blocks" (Western, 2018, para. 7). Dan Western states, "The parent-child communication influences how open you are in future relationships. There is a golden rule: better parent-child communication means fewer psychological and behavioral problems of the child in adulthood" (Western, 2018, para. 13).

However, it is not just your parents' relationship with you will affect your future relationships. It is also crucial as to what kind of relationship your parents had with each other. Toro and Taylor point out, "Although most people begin to form intimate romantic relationships in their early adulthood, much research suggests that the development of romantic intimacy traits and qualities begins in early childhood" (n.d.).

Attentive Parents

When your parents were generally attentive to you growing up, they created a nurturing and loving environment. Dan Western expresses, "When your parents love you in childhood, you know what love is and how it can be shown" (2o18, para. 10). Being raised in a loving environment increases your chances of being more confident and trusting in future romantic relationships. Your parents would naturally have fostered within you a positive self-image. They would have also encouraged you to be more comfortable expressing your feelings. Western continues, "In this case, you will not be afraid to show your love to parents, brothers and sisters, and other people who will come into your life over time" (2018, para. 10).

Neglectful, Emotionless, or Overly Cynical Parents

However, not every childhood was idyllic. If you had emotionally unavailable parents, you had neglectful parents. Emotional unavailability takes many forms, such as not giving you the love, care, and attention you deserved growing up.

With neglectful parents, you might develop insecurity and low self-esteem. "Some psychologists claim that inattentive and emotionally dramatic parents tend to raise children with lower self-esteem, children who feel more alienated, hostile, aggressive or anti-social. In other words, children who felt neglected can very often grow up as needy adults" (Western, 2018, para. 17).

You may also have difficulty trusting others and forming healthy relationships. Western suggests, "If you lack sufficient attention from one or both of your parents at an early age, you may often find yourself vying for a romantic interest's attention and often have trouble in your love life" (2018, para. 16).

Individuals with neglectful parents may suffer from often intense abandonment issues and struggle with intimacy in future relationships. You may also seek out emotionally unavailable partners—repeating the patterns you could have experienced in childhood, feeling as if that is what you deserve. "The study proved that the child unconsciously wants the parent's attention, but simply does not express it externally and eventually gets used to being stoic and inexpressive" (Western, 2018, para 20).

Parents lacking emotional expression may create a cold and distant environment. If you have parents who lack emotional expression, you may struggle with emotional intimacy in future relationships. "If the parents avoid expressing needs and desires for attention, affection, and closeness with the child, they also require such behavior from their child or children" (Western, 2018, para. 19). You may have difficulty expressing your emotions and struggle to understand others' emotions. You may also avoid emotional situations and rely on rational thinking instead of emotional expression.

Parents who are cynical about love and marriage may create a pessimistic view of relationships. If you grew up with such parents, you may have difficulty trusting others and view relationships as unstable and unreliable. "Having divorced or unmarried parents might make you either cynical about marriage or excessively cautious. You'll be reluctant to form your own family if you have an incomplete family. You consistently fear repeating your parent's fate" (Western, 2018, para. 23), meaning you may struggle with commitment and avoid long-term relationships altogether.

Chapter 3: Social Media

S ocial media is a silent thief of your time, stealing hours away from your life and leaving you with nothing but a false sense of connection and productivity.

Social media platforms keep us engaged for as long as possible, scrolling endlessly and constantly refreshing for new notifications. Being glued to our phones is a massive time sink. It is time that we could have spent on living.

While we may use social media to stay connected with friends and family, it is often superficial. Our time on social media can give us the illusion of being productive when we may not accomplish anything valuable.

It is very easy to find yourself becoming addicted to your phone and social media as an extension of it. It is important to recognize its negative impact on our lives.

Why Is Social Media So Popular?

Going about your day without being bombarded by the Internet is nearly impossible. After all, it is a global phenomenon. It is all around us. Today's fast-paced society resonates with the Internet's ability to connect us no matter where we are instantly. Social media is so popular that about "42% of the current global population of around 7.7 billion people are active social media users," which translates to roughly "3.2 billion social media users worldwide today" (Spokeo, 2019, para. 2).

Social media use is more accessible than ever. That is all thanks to the invention and subsequent success of the smartphone. To put that in perspective, about "322 million people live in the United States, 64% of whom own a smartphone" (Crevin, 2015, para. 2).

Social media is an invaluable tool for you as a teen. In your own space, you can learn to express yourself. Not only that, these apps help you stay connected with your friends while also offering you a chance to make friends all across the globe. Professors Kaveri Subrahmanyam and Patricia Greenfield report that "48 percent of online teens believe that the Internet has improved their relationships with friends" (2008, p. 126). After all, you do not have to wait until the next school day to hang out with your friend, nor do you even have to use your family's landline phone to talk to them.

As a teen, you are more vulnerable to social media's effects due to your developmental stage. Social media gives you the space for the "construction of your social identity with peer groups, especially in terms of popularity and therefore acceptance and sense of belonging" (Fabris et al., 2020, para. 2). It not only gives you a platform to share what you want when you want but also gives you the freedom of deciding what kind of content you want to engage with to "extend your network of knowledge or find and exchange information and materials" (Fabris et al., 2020, para. 2).

Social media platforms are designed to provide immediate feedback through likes, comments, and shares. This creates a sense of validation and social acceptance that can be addictive. The reward system is reinforced by algorithms prioritizing content that generates more engagement, creating a positive feedback loop. If you are a social media user yourself, think about it. How do you feel when your latest post does well? Do you feel excited when you find that your follower count is higher?

It's been "found that a certain part of the brain associated with rewards hums with activity whenever teens see one of their photos earn a lot of likes" (Almendrala, 2016, para. 3). As you become hooked on getting that buzz from the likes, you begin to use them as a measure of your self-worth—whether you are doing so consciously or not. You may even find yourself bending to various social pressures to appeal to whatever social media's current trend. The algorithm only makes it worse by blasting you with trending topics—generating even more engagement. This positive and very visible feedback can make social media addictive.

The Impact of Social Media

Social media and the Internet as a whole have a large impact on us all. Due to the very nature of how it functions, the effects of social media can be both positive and negative. There is no denying that social media can provide us with an easy platform to keep in touch with family and friends.

For many, social media can also be used as a place to distract yourself intermittently throughout the day. As a fifteen-year-old blog writer for PediMom, Suha Malik writes, "Social media can act as an escape from the real world. If a teenager is stressed, sad, or even depressed, they may turn to social media to forget their problems, even if it is only for a couple of hours. It is also a lot easier to express yourself on social media, and teens who may be shy in real life are more likely to have a bolder online presence; they can think about their words and come off as witty, even if in real life they are nothing like that at all. Additionally, teenagers may turn to social media if they feel isolated or disconnected from their family or friends" (2018, para. 9). Social media can be a great place to reach out to others without the worry of face-to-face rejection.

Despite its many benefits, social media can also negatively affect our mental health, including addiction, anxiety, and depression. One of the most negative things social media brings out is the intense fear of missing out on something considered important to you on any of your feeds. As a teen, this feeling is magnified as you do not want to be the only one in your circle of friends that missed out on seeing something happen online as soon as it happens. You want to avoid that signaled-out feeling of missing out on something. That very feeling is called fear of missing out syndrome—or FOMO. The very name makes it sound like a light-hearted or even silly concept, yet it is anything but silly. "FOMO is a very real thing. Research conducted at Duke University's Center for Advanced Hindsight found that even if you turn off notifications, you still feel anxious about missing out" (Hall, 2019, para. 5).

While it may sound a bit ridiculous, FOMO can cause some intense feelings of anxiety within certain people. "However, research also shows significant associations exist between adolescents' social media use and Fear of Missing Out (FoMO), a construct which can be defined as a pervasive apprehension that others might be having rewarding experiences from which one is absent, and it is character-ized by the desire to stay continually connected with what others are doing" (Fabris et al., 2020, para. 2).

It is shown that one of the reasons that social media is addictive is because of the intense worry of missing out on something. It breeds obsession—because it makes you think, oh I just have to refresh my feed one more time. It might make you more inclined to look through all your social media feeds as the first thing you do after you wake up. Malik says, "One of the first reasons that come to mind when talking about why our generation is addicted to social media is probably… FOMO. While some don't care if they are the first ones to see a new post by someone popular in their school, or even a celebrity, teens often pay a lot of attention to their phones so they can see and under-stand what is going on in the world in terms of pop culture" (2018, para. 2). It is the very mechanism that helps you try to feel in control of staying up to date with everything that could be going on in school among all your friends and peers. "FOMO is one of the main reasons why many teenagers feel the compulsive need to spend a decent chunk of their time on social media; to make sure they are up to date with all happenings to fit in" (Malik, 2018, para. 4).

Another very addictive and potentially harmful aspect of social media is the like system of platforms such as Instagram. Social media platforms are designed to keep users engaged and returning for more. "An observational study showed that spending more than a few hours per week using electronic media correlated negatively with self-report-ed happiness, life satisfaction, and self-esteem, whereas time spent on non-screen activities (in-person social interactions, sports or exercise, print media, homework, religious services, working at a paid job) cor-related positively with psychological well-being, among adolescents. Other observational studies have linked spending more than 2 hours daily on social networking sites and personal electronic devices with high rates of suicidality and depressive symptoms among adolescent girls. However, youth who sustained high levels of face-to-face socializing were relatively protected against the negative consequences of too much time online" (Abi-Jaoude et al., 2020, p. E137).

The reward system, where every like, comment, or share provides a dopamine hit, creates a sense of satisfaction and social acceptance. This positive feedback reinforces the desire to continue using social media, leading to a cycle of addiction. "This addiction can cause them to fall into a cycle of only finding happiness from this source, and when they see that some of their friends have been accomplishing things in real life, it can lead to jealousy. These people that rely on social media are the same people who will be running into issues later on when they figure out that the skills and bad habits they developed are non-transferable in the workforce. As a result, they never fully involve themselves with their peers and lack the proper communication skills necessary to function" (Crevin, 2015, para. 8). Becoming obsessive over follower counts and likes can also lead to a focus on external validation—which in turn can have a negative impact on self-esteem. This can lead to social media providing pressure to conform to specific beauty standards and success, negatively impacting mental health.

Social media addiction can negatively impact mental health, such as anxiety, depression, and social isolation. "Other studies also have observed links between high levels of social media use and depression or anxiety symptoms. A 2016 study of more than 450 teens found that greater social media use, nighttime social media use, and emotional investment in social media—such as feeling upset when prevented from logging on—were each linked with worse sleep quality and higher anxiety levels and depression" (Mayo Clinic Staff, 2022, para. 4). "Stress related to life on social media, particularly the fear of being neglected by one's online social network, seems to fuel dependence on social media platforms. This type of stress would therefore seem to be reflected in problematic or excessive use of social media, possibly aimed at maintaining or increasing one's online relationships, satisfying adolescents' need to belong to a peer group" (Fabris et al., 2020, para. 10).

Social media platforms can be a breeding ground for trolling and bullying. Online anonymity can embolden people to say hurtful things they would not say in person, leading to a false sense of reality and potentially serious consequences. Cyberbullying, in particular, is a major issue, and it can take many forms, such as harassment, humiliation, or exclusion. This type of behavior can have a significant impact on mental health, leading to anxiety, depression, and even suicide. "Cyberbullying illustrates how traditional offline adolescent issues are moving to the electronic stage. A questionnaire study of eighty-four thirteen- to eighteen-year-old teens found that text messages were the most common form of electronic bullying. Most importantly, the findings suggest that students' role as victims and perpetrators of bullying in the offline world predicted their role in electronic bullying. Although a subset of traditional bullies were victims in the virtual world, there was no indication that victims of bullying in the real world retaliated by becoming bullies on the Internet or in text messages" (Subrahmanyam & Greenfield, 2008, p. 128).

In addition to cyberbullying, social media has also been linked to other harms, including identity theft and the spread of misinformation. Identity theft involves the malicious use of personal information, which can be stolen and used for fraud. Conversely, misinformation involves spreading false or misleading information, which can lead to confusion, division, and even harm. "Electronic communication forms also differ in the extent to which their content is public or private and in the extent to which users can keep content private. Public chat rooms and bulletin boards are perhaps the least private. Users' screen names are publicly available, although they choose their screen names and whether their profile is public or private. Of course, private conversations between users are not publicly available, and such private messages are typically restricted to other users who have also registered. This restriction precludes lurkers and others not registered with the site from privately contacting a user" (Subrahmanyam & Greenfield, 2008, p. 122).

Social media is a breeding ground for poor language skills. Online people tend to rely heavily on shorthand. Social media is often used for informal communication, which may involve abbreviations, emoticons, and slang. This can lead to a decrease in traditional language skills, spelling, and grammar. Crevin points out that "people tend to forget that the English language is neglected while online. It tends to get swept under the rug when they are online" (2015, para. 7). When you write to your friends online, it's almost as if you are using another language with each other. Maybe sometimes you communicate without saying anything at all. Crevin says, "People use shorthand and shortened versions of the words to convey a message much quicker. This does not necessarily negatively affect how we communicate because written language tends to be easier to decipher. People will run encounter issues when they try to integrate these forms of communication into the daily language; it lowers their social skills when they use those kinds of words and phrases because they cannot properly convey what they need to these days without using some sort of speech that is every day or not in a reputable dictionary" (2015, para. 7).

Internet slang and jargon only become a problem when you start to use them in your everyday life. It is also inappropriate to try and use this internet to speak in your academic papers for either high school or college. "It leads people to try and shoehorn our colloquial metaphors into daily conversations and use the slang terms that social media has helped develop, form, and popularize in the mainstream media. This has shaped a society that no longer functions healthily in social situations" (Crevin, 2015, para. 7).

Therefore, it is important to strike a balance between the positive and negative effects of social media. You can achieve balance by setting boundaries on social media usage, such as limiting screen time and avoiding comparisons with others on social media. Avoiding comparisons with others and cultivating a positive self-image can help mitigate the adverse effects of the reward system. Prioritizing real-life relationships, such as spending time with family and friends, can also help maintain a healthy perspective on social media.

The Disruption of Social Media

There is no denying that social media has become a distraction. It has been linked to a decrease in our attention spans. Social media is designed to keep users engaged and returning for more—which makes you want to consume more and more content at a quicker rate. With prolonged social media usage, you will soon find it very hard to concentrate on anything for long. Baptist Health points out, "In our age of quickly evolving technology and social media, it is no wonder that adults and children are having difficulty focusing their attention. Considering smartphones, email, TV, video games, the internet, and social media, we can easily see why our brain's neurons are constant. These technological advances give us more access to screen time, and the ability to access social media on any device increases the amount of time we spend on social platforms" (2020, para. 1).

"The constant ability to access social media and fast-paced technology means our brains are exposed to high brain stimulation, and our neurons are firing all day. This easy access to social media on multiple devices leads to multi-tasking, inhibiting our ability to focus on one task at a time" (Baptist Health, 2020, para. 2).

As a student, social media can affect your academic performance. Social media usage during class time or studying can interfere with concentration and retention of information. Students who spend more time on social media have lower academic performance than those who spend less. Students like to stream music from different online streaming platforms, like Spotify or SoundCloud, while they study or do their assignments. Students will argue that having something to listen to that they enjoy helps them feel better about doing their work, making it more likely for them to complete it. However, it becomes a distraction when you become more worried about the songs you pick to listen to or begin singing or dancing to the music (Angelastro, 2015, para. 14).

Students are more inclined to want various mental simulations during class and find it harder and harder to sit through long class periods. "Students are used to shorter clips and videos from social media. They have developed the habit of using social media during class while learning remotely and are accustomed to quick and instant access to information on these platforms" (Kim et al., 2021, para. 10).

Think about the last time you had to sit still for a class period. Did the teacher honestly hold your whole attention for the entire period? When you do your homework, are you completely focused? Or do you find that your mind is wondering about what's going on in your social media feeds? "Now, students cannot sit through a full hour and a half lecture and fully pay attention. From her own experience, Dr. King has found that she can only hold students' focus for about 5-10 minutes at a time before they become distracted by their phones and that they learn better in 5-10 minute bytes. As a result, she has had to modify her lectures and ensure enough pauses in between to keep her students engaged. While social media does not directly decrease attention span, chronic use of social media while attempting to multitask does. It contributes to an increased need for stimulation and decreased ability to absorb lots of information" (Kim et al., 2021, para. 11).

Social media can also negatively impact face-to-face communication. If you are using the Internet for communication for too long, it can lead to a decline in social skills and an inability to connect with others physically. Matt Crevin points out, "Since it has become more prevalent, social media has made people want to interact with people online rather than in person because it has simplified the process. A simpler process allows things to be done easier and more efficiently, attracting more people to try it" (2015, para. 4). It makes sense; social media has made it easy to make new friends. You can interact with someone without any fear of rejection directly to your face. You may not be so nervous when interacting anymore with your friends or your crush if you talk to them over the Internet instead of talking to them face-to-face. However, Crevin goes on to say, "Although it may be viewed as a positive change, this has caused people to become more antisocial than ever, as counterintuitive as that may sound" (2015, para . 4).

Social Media: The Fake Reality

Social media platforms create a sense of false intimacy by encouraging users to share personal details and emotions with a broader audience. This can lead to a closeness based on something other than genuine connection or interaction. People may also feel they know someone well simply because they follow them on social media, leading to a false sense of intimacy.

Social media platforms encourage users to compare themselves to others, leading to a culture of comparison. This can lead to feelings of inadequacy, low self-esteem, and depression. People may also present a false image of themselves on social media, leading to a distorted sense of reality. "Measuring oneself against others comes naturally for the human mind. In some ways, it can be helpful by inspiring motivation to improve yourself or boost your self-esteem. On the other hand, comparisons can be harmful when they leave you feeling inferior or depressed. The latter is often the case regarding comparisons drawn via social media. People generally like to share peak experiences, flattering images, and positive news about themselves. These highly curated slices of reality are human highlight reels masquerading as normal, ho-hum moments of everyday life" (Spokeo, 2021, para. 12).

This can create a sense of social pressure to conform to specific standards of beauty or success, leading to anxiety and depression. Trying to hold yourself to someone else's curated image is impossible. "Bottom line: One cannot judge another based solely on how they appear on social media. Instagram will show the happy bits of their lives in little squares, and Snapchat will capture their outings with their friends and family. It is doubtful for someone to illustrate their weak points and struggles for the world to see; remember this next time it seems as if someone has everything going for them and that perfect life" (Evenosky, 2016, para. 1).

Even though it's natural, given the competitive nature of social media, the question is, why do we do it? "Why are we constantly on a mission to prove to others that we do fun things and that our lives are exciting? Is social media solely a place to express ourselves, or has it served as a reason to "beat ourselves up," to create a false image for how we want to be portrayed to our followers and friends, and to prove to ourselves that we can be equal to the one with five million followers" (Evenosky, 2016, para. 2)?

Social media can create cognitive dissonance and discomfort when holding conflicting beliefs or values. For example, someone may post about environmental issues on social media but engage in environmentally damaging activities in real life. This can lead to feelings of hypocrisy and can create a false sense of reality.

Social media platforms do not require users to have face-to-face interactions, leading to a lack of eye-to-eye contact. This can create a sense of detachment and prevent people from truly understanding one another. It can also create a fake reality, as people may present themselves differently in person than online. "The number of face-to-face interactions is not the only thing negatively impacted. The quality of these decreasing interactions is suffering as well. People are not having these intimate conversations and personal interactions with each other anymore. People, instead, have turned to the Internet to take away some of the nervousness that some may find in trying to start a relationship with another person. Social media is a driving force behind these changes. These sites want people to use them as frequently as possible. When they see that they could get more traffic from those people having interactions with their online resource, they jump at the chance to take advantage of the situation" (Crevin, 2015, para. 4).

Life Without Social Media

Even though it may be impossible to imagine, life without using social media is possible. It may seem daunting at first. After all, you have grown up in a world where social media and the Internet have been around you since birth. It is everywhere, and that is by design. "Social media is so ingrained in our society that life without it seems unimaginable" (Acosta, 2021, para. 18).

Social media constantly bombards you for your attention. "Constantly hearing the distracting beeps of notifications can create anxiety and cause you to jump back on social media. Eliminating those notifications will get you used to staying away from your social media for longer periods" (Hall, 2019, para. 16). The lack of notifications might initially feel alarming, but you will soon grow to appreciate the silence.

"Without social media, life would inevitably vary. Interacting with someone would have to be in person. It would mean less time surfing on social networks and more time spent in real life. Asking someone to hang out via social networks sounds easier, and in case you get rejected, you probably will not feel that hurt. However, asking someone out in real life makes you feel jittery. Facial expressions are seen, the cracking sound of your voice is heard, and the beating rhythm of your heart can be felt. It is always easier to play it off behind the screen than face it out in reality" (Santally, 2018, para. 3).

You can start breaking yourself of your social media usage by setting usage rules for yourself. You can start by limiting screen time if you want to take it slow. "Before you insist that you cannot quit cold turkey, rest assured that this is a temporary measure" (Chantim, 2020, para. 3). But if you can handle the cold turkey method, you can take a break from social media altogether. It is also essential to be mindful of the content we consume and create on social media. You should avoid comparisons with others to help cultivate a positive self-image. You should also be taking steps to protect your personal information, such as using strong passwords and avoiding sharing sensitive information o nline.

Setting time limits for social media use can be a helpful way to create balance in our lives. We can allocate specific times of day to check social media; outside of those times, we can focus on other activities that bring us joy and fulfillment. It might be helpful if you have someone else to help you wean off social media. "Whether you want to get fit, lose weight, or spend less time on social media, having someone to hold you accountable can make all the difference. Find a loved one interested in detoxing with you, and then discuss how both of you plan on following through" (Chantim, 2020, para. 4). Andra Chantim goes on "that the people closest to you know you better than you know yourself. So, ask your loved ones what they have noticed about your relationship with your phone. You may discover you have unwittingly picked up some bad tendencies, like checking your phone mid-conversation or texting at the dinner table" (2020, para. 6). It will also be helpful to detox from social media and excessive phone use by setting rules during nighttime. "Tell yourself that after a particular hour, your phone goes into its charging station and is out of commission until the next day. Move your charging station from your bedside table to an area out of arm's reach. You should stop using your phone as your alarm clock" (Chantim, 2020, para. 11).

If you struggle with getting off social media, there are a couple of tricks you can use to help you. Chantim suggests a trick of even putting a simple rubber band around your phone when it's not time to use it. It is a simple notion, but "the simple trick can help you stop mindlessly picking up your device" (Chantim, 2020, para. 7). Chantim suggests another trick "Putting social media apps into a separate folder creates one extra step you have to take to access them, which can help you cut down on mindless clicking. After all, you are more likely to click on those social media icons when they're on your home screen" (2020, para. 13).

You can also use phone applications to help you see where you sink most of your time on your phone. "Download an app like Moment (available on iOS and Android) that helps you break down how much time you spend on your apps. If you are one user, you are likely already familiar with your device's built-in screen time feature. Instead of looking at your daily average, which factors in email and other work-related phone usages, check out your list of "Most Used" apps and see how much time you devote to specific social media apps" (Chantim, 2020, para. 5).

You can also try to ask yourself questions anytime you pick up your phone. Chantim suggests the following questions: What for? Why now? What else? The questions remind you to question whether or not you picked up your phone with purpose" (2020, para. 8).

Social media is often used as an escape from the monotony of life. "We often find ourselves on our phones or laptops to escape life, and when life without social media begins, it can feel like we are stuck in one place with nowhere to go. It took me a while to realize that life without social media means more freedom, and life online is not the only place where we can find happiness. Life offline is not all bad—it is just different from life online" (Acosta, 2021, para 62).

Once you quit social media, you must figure out a new way to deal with your desire to escape. As writer Elise Acosta points out, "When life without social media is done right, you become more focused on what is important in life and less worried about the things that do not matter" (2021, para. 26). Without social media, we can also improve our focus. Social media is designed to monopolize your attention through constant notifications and alerts. However, without the constant distractions of social media, we can concentrate on the task at hand and achieve our goals more efficiently. There are many benefits to disconnecting from social media and living in the moment.

"Life gets easier without all the distractions: there are no longer any thoughts related to likes, retweets, or followers. When life without social media becomes your reality, it is easy to focus on living" (Acosta, 2021, para. 28).

One way to embrace life without social media is through meditation. Meditation can help reduce stress and anxiety, increase focus, and promote inner peace. It allows you to disconnect from the world's noise and focus on your thoughts and emotions, which can be challenging when constantly scrolling through social media feeds. "In addition to helping you manage stress and sleep better, meditation can help you be more mindful of what you're doing, including how you're using social media (Chantim, 2020, para. 14). To check out more information about meditation, there are websites you can visit such as: www.marketshop73.online/genie-script

Another benefit of disconnecting from social media is connecting with family and friends on a deeper level. When we are not constantly checking our phones and scrolling through social media feeds, we can give our full attention to the people around us. We can engage in meaningful conversations and create memories that will last a lifetime. "A world without social media allows you more time to meet and get to know people. Of course, your phone will no longer be the first thing you look for in the morning or the last thing at night. During hanging out moments, you feel more present without social media because you do not have to constantly photograph everything; instead, you live the moment and enjoy it, and you rely on your memory to remind you how memorable it was" (Santally, 2018, para. 7). In place of social media, we can pick up a phone and call a friend or family member. This can be a great way to reconnect with someone we have not talked to and create a deeper connection than a social media message or comment ever could.

Self-discipline is also an essential aspect of life without social media. It can be easy to get sucked into the endless scroll of social media feeds, but without that distraction, we can focus on our goals and priorities. "We are taught from a young age to be aware of how much cash we are spending, but we do not think twice about how much time we spend on social media" (Chantim, 2020, para. 9). We can create healthy habits and routines that promote well-being and personal growth. "If your social media use is seriously hindering your productivity, but you need help to resist, consider an app like Freedom, suggests Price. You can set up blocks of time you want, have the Freedom to block social media apps, and even enable a "Locked Mode," which will not allow you to cancel those time limits—no matter how much you beg" (Chantim, 2020, para. 12).

Writing is another way to embrace life without social media. Writing in a journal can help us process our thoughts and emotions and even spark creativity. We can also write letters to friends and family members, which can be a thoughtful and personal way to communicate. If you are interested in writing, try investing in a mediation journal. A suggested journal can be found at this website: www.marketshop73.online/meditation-journal

Life without social media can seem daunting, but it can also be a time of self-discovery, growth, and connection. "After quitting social media, you will find that you can focus on a given task until it is done, which will inevitably make you more productive and efficient with your work" (Hall, 2019, para 22).

Chapter 4: Teens and Drugs

Lila had always struggled with anxiety and depression. Still, she felt no one understood her pain's depth. She tried talking to her friends and family about her struggles, but she always thought they dismissed her feelings or told her to "just cheer up."

One day, at a party, Lila tried marijuana for the first time. As she took a hit from the joint, she felt a wave of relaxation wash over her. For the first time in a long time, she felt like she could breathe without the weight of anxiety crushing her chest.

After that night, Lila began smoking marijuana more frequently. Whenever she felt overwhelmed by her emotions, she would light up and let the drugs take the edge off. She convinced herself she was just using it as a coping mechanism but was masking her hidden pain.

Over time, Lila's drug use escalated. She started smoking before work and school and began using harder drugs like cocaine and ecstasy.

While the drugs provided temporary relief, they worsened her mental health and caused more problems.

It was not until Lila hit rock bottom and checked herself into rehab that she realized the depth of her pain. Through therapy and support from loved ones, she was able to address the root causes of her anxiety and depression and learn healthier coping mechanisms. In addition, Lila realized that drugs were only masking her pain, not helping her heal.

Drug use can have various reasons, one of which is to numb or avoid hidden emotional pain. Many people turn to drugs as a coping mechanism to deal with trauma, loss, or other emotional distress. While drugs may temporarily relieve, they often exacerbate the underlying issue, leading to more significant problems.

Getting high on drugs can mask hidden pain and lead to a cycle of avoidance and escalation. Individuals who use drugs to cope may experience short-term relief but become more isolated, anxious, and depressed.

Recognizing the connection between drug use and emotional pain is essential, and addressing the issue head-on rather than turning to drugs is a temporary solution. Individuals can find long-term relief and build a healthier, more meaningful life.

How Drugs Affect Your Life

There's no denying drug abuse causes many problems. Depending on what drug is abused, you may experience respiratory problems, heart disease, liver damage, kidney damage, or any other major health issues. For example, using inhalants such as glue or paint can cause permanent damage to the brain and other organs, leading to long-term health problems. Using tobacco products such as cigarettes or vaping devices can increase the risk of lung cancer, heart disease, and other serious health problems. Drugs can also weaken your immune system, making it more difficult for individuals to fight infections and illnesses. If you are immunocompromised, that would be even more dangerous for you

Even if you are only 'misusing' drugs, you can suffer many adverse effects. The AspenRidge Recovery Center warns: "Left untreated, continued substance misuse can critically impact physical health-damaging both the mind and the body. The negative effects of substance misuse can include:

- Experiencing circulation problems

- Organ failure

- Digestive problems

- Fatigue

- Sleep disruptions

- Increase in suicidal thoughts

- Irrational thinking

- Experiencing depression and anxiety

- Tolerance and dependence on drugs" (2022, para. 8).

These are all very negative effects of using drugs. People use drugs to escape the pain of their daily lives. AspenRidge Recovery Center recognizes that when they say, "Many who suffer from substance use disorder experience entering a cycle of negativity. From physical symptoms of lack of sleep and increased fatigue, they may become irritable; this can become a catalyst for performing poorly at work due to a lack of concentration" (2022, para. 10). This negativity cycle can only lead to more abuse as you poorly cope with all the parts of your life that are falling apart.

Drug abuse can strain relationships with family, friends, and romantic partners. Individuals who abuse drugs may become isolated and withdraw, leading to feelings of loneliness and depression. They may also experience conflict with loved ones due to new erratic behavior, financial problems, or other issues associated with substance abuse. In some cases, drug abuse can lead to the breakdown of relationships altogether, as partners or friends may not want to be around the person abusing drugs.

The AspenRidge Recovery Center states that drug abuse has many different social impacts. They are as follows:

- "Breakdown of intimate relationships

- Lack of respect and trust

- Lack of commitment in other relationships

- Legal implications after an outburst of negative behavior

- Lack of interest in previous hobbies" (2022, para. 11).

Drug abuse can also impact academic performance. Students who abuse drugs may struggle with attendance, miss assignments, and perform poorly on tests. They may also experience memory and concentration problems, making learning and retaining new information more challenging. Substance abuse can also lead to disciplinary action and expulsion from school, which can have long-term consequences.

Drug use can impair memory and learning in teenagers. If their memory becomes impaired, it will be difficult for them to succeed in school and other areas of life. For example, marijuana use can affect short-term memory, making it harder for teenagers to retain the information they have just learned. This lack of knowledge retention can impact their ability to perform well in school, leading to lower grades and potentially limiting their future opportunities.

Impact on Brain Function

The brain is one of the most important organs in our body, responsible for controlling our thoughts, emotions, and behaviors. Drugs have a significant impact on your brain's function, leading to a variety of negative consequences.

The developing teenage brain is highly vulnerable to the detrimental effects of drugs. According to NIDA, research has shown that drug use can change the brain's structure and function, particularly in decision-making, memory, and impulse control (2020, p. 11). These changes can have long-lasting effects on brain function, even after a person stops using drugs. Therefore, for individuals struggling with drug use, early intervention can help prevent further damage to the brain and improve the overall quality of life. For instance, drugs can disrupt the growth of the prefrontal cortex, which is responsible for decision-making and impulse control, potentially resulting in impulsive behavior and poor decision-making abilities that can negatively impact the teenager's future (NIDA, 2020, p. 16). For instance, teenagers under the influence of alcohol or drugs may be unable to drive safely, increasing their chances of accidents, injuries, and legal issues. Drug use can lead to other risky behaviors such as unsafe sexual practices, heightening the risks of health problems, and other consequences.

Teenagers who use drugs are at higher risk of developing addiction later in life. Addiction is a chronic disease that affects the brain and can have serious consequences on a person's physical and mental health, as well as their relationships and ability to function in society. Using opioids such as heroin or prescription painkillers can lead to physical dependence, which can be difficult to overcome without professional treatment.

Abusing drugs can significantly impact a person's mental health. Teenagers who use drugs are also at a heightened risk of developing mental health problems, including depression, anxiety, and psychosis. If you are already diagnosed with any mental health illness, drug abuse can exacerbate mental health issues, making them even more challenging to manage. It can lead to the development of mental health issues such as depression, anxiety, and paranoia. The use of drugs can affect the brain's reward system, leading to addiction and compulsive drug-seeking behavior. For example, stimulants such as cocaine or methamphetamine can cause paranoia, anxiety, and depression.

AspenRidge Recovery Center states: "Not only do drugs work to interact directly with the body causing such effects as the above, but many also directly interact with the central nervous system, which has acute psychological effects that negatively impact mental health. Some symptoms of mental impacts include:

- Reduction of cognitive abilities

- Memory loss

- Increased cravings

- Lack of concentration and focus

- Poor decision-making" (2022, para. 9).

At-Risk Teens

Adolescence is a challenging time for many teenagers; some are more at risk for negative outcomes than others.

Low self-esteem is a common issue among teenagers and can put them at risk for negative consequences. You may feel insecure about your abilities, appearance, or social status if you have low self-esteem. When you struggle with your self-image, it can lead to depression, anxiety, and social isolation. During those times of isolation and mental hardship, you are more likely to engage in risky behaviors—such as drug abuse—to cope with your inadequacy.

If you have a lack of parental supervision, it can also put you at risk. Without parental guidance, you may be more likely to engage in risky behaviors because you feel you can get away with it.

Bullying is a significant problem that puts you at risk for using drugs. Feeling signaled out at school or among your group of friends makes you feel isolated and overwhelmed with other horrible feelings. You may then start to seek out drugs or engage in other risky behaviors to try and cope with the pain you are feeling.

Struggling with school may also put you at risk of developing risky behaviors. For example, if you find yourself constantly struggling with your classes or your homework, you may begin to feel very discouraged. If you continue to fail and struggle, you may turn to drugs to distract yourself from the disappointment. This is very hard on students as you know that these years at high school can determine what college you get into—further worsening any feelings of hopelessness and despair.

It is important to be aware of these things that can trigger risky behavior as a coping mechanism. Knowing potential triggers can help you avoid using them for yourself. It is also good to be aware of these issues if your friends struggle.

Why Do Teens Do Drugs?

While the reasons for drug use among teenagers can vary, some common factors can contribute to this behavior. Children who grow up in households where drug use is normalized may be more likely to experiment with drugs themselves. Additionally, if you are experiencing issues at home, such as neglect or abuse, you may turn to drugs as a coping mechanism.

Peer pressure is another factor that can influence teens to use drugs. Your friends may pressure you to use drugs to fit in or be accepted. You might also see your friends doing drugs and want to try it for yourself out of sheer curiosity. You may want to try drugs to see what they do or how they feel. Unfortunately, this curiosity can quickly lead to addiction and severe health problems if you aren't careful.

You can simply turn to drugs to feel good. Drugs can provide a temporary escape from negative feelings and stress. Many drugs are known for causing a euphoric feeling, which is a high that people seek when they want a quick fix to feel good. Ryan Michaels points out that our brain has no off switch, so "we are often plagued by unpleasant thoughts and feelings that are tempting to escape. We learn that drugs and alcohol do a decent job of turning down the noise of daily life, allowing us to focus on other things or nothing at all. They are a quick and easy fix, making them all the more seductive" (2020, para. 2).

Some people may use drugs to ease their physical or emotional pain. Painkillers, for example, can help with chronic pain or recovering from surgery or an injury. Some people who suffer from mental health issues—like depression or anxiety—may self-medicate themselves by using drugs. Unfortunately, drug use can also exacerbate depression and other mental health problems, leading to a cycle of substance abuse and worsening mental health.

The Escape Habit

Drugs are very attractive because they are the quintessential escape for those who are suffering. If you feel overwhelmed, anxious, or depressed, you might turn to drugs, alcohol, or other unhealthy behaviors, to numb your feelings or avoid dealing with your problems or responsibilities. Or perhaps you also suffer from an intense sense of boredom with life. "If your main reason for using drugs or alcohol is to escape, it will catch up to you. You are on the road to a real problem, and you are probably better off getting clean" (Michaels, 2020, para. 6).

Michaels understands those issues. He writes, "We all wish we could mentally check out some days. Sometimes days run together without excitement. The minutiae of everyday life, all the little tasks that must be done to keep ourselves fed, clothed, and safe from the elements, are often exhausting" (2020, para. 1). Sometimes everyday life can wear on you. Sometimes just going through the motions of life can be very, very tiring—especially if you find yourself struggling with other issues. Michaels stresses, "Then the major events cause us additional pain and uncertainty: a broken-down vehicle, sudden unemployment, and a nasty breakup. With so many responsibilities, stresses, and disappointments, is it any wonder that humans enjoy the escape that drugs and alcohol can temporarily provide" (2020, para. 1)?

Learning to feel and process uncomfortable emotions is another crucial step in breaking the escape habit. Rather than trying to avoid or numb complicated feelings, learning how to sit with those feelings and process them healthily is essential. Michaels says, "This is the big one. The allure (but also the problem) of drugs and alcohol is that you can push away those uncomfortable feelings of boredom, stress, loneliness, anger, etc., without addressing them. However, it is only a temporary fix. Wake up the next day, and the issues are still there—only now you have added a hangover" (2020, para. 13). He is correct. If you use drugs to push away your sadness, you are not addressing the sadness. Instead, you are simply burying it. If anything, you are only adding to those feelings that are causing you pain.

"Learning to accept and feel uncomfortable feelings is important in sobriety, but it is not easy. It takes conscious effort. Urge surfing is one method you can try. The basic premise is that you allow yourself to feel the craving fully. When you accept your feelings, the craving often dissipates" (Michaels, 2020, para. 14). It is important to know if a pattern in your behavior draws you to drugs. What causes your cravings? Michaels continues, "Urge surfing helps put your cravings into perspective. What is a craving anyway? What happens if you do not give in to it? Will you explode? If you can learn to sit with craving and accept it, you will find it has no power over you and will dissipate on its own" (2020, para. 15).

Learning to Live Without Drugs

Learning to live without drugs is difficult, but it is possible if you are committed to the process. Sobriety will mean coming to terms with many things, and some of those things may be very difficult to process. But it is worth it. After all, "A sober life is worth living. It is a fully felt, fully experienced life" (Michaels, 2020, para. 21). Michaels warns, "There is no getting around it; the first few sober weeks will be uncomfortable. Not only will you experience the physical withdrawal of the drug, but you will also realize how much extra time you now have. For me, getting loaded was the main event of the day. All the Netflix and social media I did under the influence were mindless, passive activities. When I got sober, those things did not appeal to me anymore. Sitting alone in my house each night with nothing to do was torture" (2020, para. 9). Sobriety means living; it is a much better life than being a slave to your drug addiction.

If you are serious about fighting drug addiction, you must know you cannot do it alone. You need to reach out to someone to help you. That somebody can be a trusted loved one, family member, friend, or even a support group.

"The journey to recovery is tough and requires support from loved ones. Hence, though the effects can be damaging, it is never too late to turn over a new leaf and rebuild bridges. The first step to recovery is recognizing the signs of substance abuse and getting the relevant help, whether for yourself or someone you care for" (AspenRidge Recovery Center, 2022, para. 13).

Having someone helps to hold you accountable for fighting the addiction. They will help you with every step along the way. It is essential to find people who understand what you are going through and can offer guidance and support as you navigate the recovery process. It would also be beneficial to "find a community of other sober people to lean on" (Michaels, 2020, para. 12). A community like that will lend you valuable insights on overcoming addiction. They will be able to give you firsthand knowledge of how the process will undoubtedly be hard but more than worth it in the end.

When dealing with overcoming addiction, it is important to learn how to structure your day better. Setting your schedule means having devoted time for everything—like setting a regular sleep schedule, eating healthy meals regularly, engaging in regular exercise, and other self-care activities. Setting and holding yourself accountable to your structured schedule can help you stay focused and avoid falling into old behavior patterns. However, a schedule cannot be the only tool in your recovery toolbox. As Michaels warns, "The suggestion above is only a short-term strategy. You will not be able to distract yourself forever. You need to develop a new sense of purpose for sobriety to stick. You need to change your outlook. You will need to identify your triggers. You will need hobbies and a daily routine" (2020, para. 11).

Setting and working toward goals can be important to learn to live without drugs. This might mean setting small, achievable goals for yourself, such as going for a walk each day or attending a support group meeting, or it might mean setting larger goals, such as going back to school or pursuing a new career. Setting and working towards goals can help you stay motivated and focused on the future, giving you a sense of accomplishment and purpose as you progress in your recovery.

You will also keep busy to keep yourself clean. When you have a full schedule of activities, you are less likely to have time or energy to engage in unhealthy behaviors. Michaels says, "Drugs and alcohol gave me something to look forward to at the end of the day. The thing about addiction is that, at a certain point, instead of using a substance to enhance activity, substance use becomes the activity. You do not have to worry about pursuing other interests" (2020, para. 4). This might mean taking up a new sport or hobby, volunteering in your community, or finding other ways to stay active and engaged.

Self-care and self-love are crucial for embracing sobriety. This might mean taking care of your physical health by eating well and getting enough exercise or relaxing and unwinding each day to prioritize your well-being and engage in activities that bring you joy and fulfillment. "Let me state the obvious: drug and alcohol use is unhealthy. They wreak havoc on the brain and body. The best way to counter the destructive nature of addiction is to flip that destruction on its head by treating your brain and body with kindness. It becomes much harder to justify ingesting poisons when you habitually treat yourself well" (Michaels, 2020, para. 18). If you are treating yourself well, you will want to succeed and not relapse.

For some people, exploring spirituality can be essential to recovery. For some, it is very helpful to practice meditation or mindfulness, attend religious services, or engage in other spiritual practices that help you connect with something larger than yourself. Developing spirituality can help you find meaning and purpose and offer comfort and support during difficult times.

Doctor Lance Dodes notes that addiction is an emotional problem (2015, para. 1). However, he is a little more reluctant to say that it is a spiritual one. He notes, "Of course, sometimes people, including people with addictions, feel less distressed when they feel "spiritually" at peace—comfortable with themselves and their place in the universe. But that does not mean that addiction is a spiritual problem, or that addiction treatment has anything to do with becoming more spiritual" (2015). And it is true. It makes sense. One does feel more at peace when you feel more comfortable. He continues, "Addiction is not a spiritual problem. Indeed, saying that it has caused many a great deal of pain. Addiction is hard enough for people without having to think they have shallow or tormented souls" (Dodes, 2015, para. 8).

Learning to love life fully is important to break the addiction habit. Learning to embrace all the ups and downs that come with life and finding joy and meaning in every moment will help you realize that you do not need to always turn to drugs. Loving life also means working towards long-term recovery. Long-term recovery is crucial to sobriety, where you work with either a therapist or a treatment program to learn healthy ways to cope with the stresses in your life that made you turn to drugs in the first place.

Chapter 5: Peer Pressure

One day, a teenage girl named Lily was hanging out with her friends. They were all laughing and having a good time until one of the girls suggested they all try smoking marijuana. Lily had never tried drugs before and was hesitant, but she didn't want to seem uncool, or risk being excluded from the group.

As the joint made its way around the circle, Lily felt increasingly uncomfortable. She didn't like how the drug made her feel but didn't want to disappoint her friends or be seen as weak. So, she continued to smoke even though it made her feel sick and dizzy.

After the group dispersed, Lily went home feeling ashamed of herself. Deep down, she knew she didn't want to smoke marijuana, but the fear of losing her friends had overridden her better judgment. She couldn't stop thinking about how peer pressure had made her do something she didn't want to, and she felt like she had lost a bit of herself in the process.

This experience made Lily realize the dangers of peer pressure and the importance of being true to oneself. She vowed never to let anyone else's opinions or actions again dictate her choices. While it was a difficult lesson to learn, it helped her become more confident and secure in her identity.

From a young age, we value the opinions of those around us. We seek validation from our parents, teachers, and peers, often prioritizing their approval over our instincts and desires. While seeking guidance and feedback from others can be helpful, it can also lead to a dangerous trap: peer pressure.

Peer pressure is the influence that our social circle has on our thoughts, feelings, and behaviors. It can manifest in many forms, from subtle comments about our appearance or interests to more overt pressure to engage in risky behaviors like substance use or bullying.

As a teen, peer pressure can be especially dangerous. You are in a period of your life where you are trying to find your place in the world and figure out who you are. It is a time of experimentation, exploration, and growth. But when the opinions of your peers become too loud, those opinions can compromise your values.

How Does Peer Pressure Affect Teen Development?

Peer pressure is a powerful force that can significantly impact your development. As you navigate the challenges of adolescence, you will be confronted with social pressures to conform to certain behaviors, beliefs, and attitudes. You have heard the phrase peer pressure before. But the term isn't necessarily good or bad on its own. Doctor Jenni Jacobsen points out the dichotomy by saying, "Sometimes, peer pressure can result in unhealthy or dangerous behaviors, but it can also influence teens positively, such as encouraging them to put forth their best effort in school" (2017, para. 5). Anna Almendrala, senior reporter for the HuffPost, agrees by calling it agnostic, suggesting that it exists mostly as something good, with the undeniable potential to be bad. Almendrala then stresses that what you see online—what your peers post and like—matters most in terms of peer pressure (2016, para. 4).

During your adolescent years, you will experience the most pressure from your peers. Your friends might have influenced you when you were young, but it is different once you turn thirteen. It is said that "while as a teen you might feel like you have grown up, but your brain is still developing, and one of its immature functions is judgment" (Scripps, 2019, para. 7). Jacobsen says, "Teens and peer pressure are a common combination, with peer pressure statistics showing that when teens' friends ask them to smoke or drink, they are more likely to do so. One peer pressure definition describes it as occurring when a teen does something they normally would not do to fit in with friends" (2017, para. 2).

When you are a teen, it's easy to get caught up in the world around you—especially if you try hard to fit in with a new group of friends. Joel Smith says, "Every destructive influence has a touch of appeal that tantalizes our senses. It is just enough to get us interested" (2018, para. 8). It makes a lot of sense that it might particularly grab you if a group of peers seems cool that you will be instantly attached to them. Mystery and danger are like magnets. "Every world religion, political view, or philosophy of life can tempt our allegiance. Identifying where we fail to line up with reality can be difficult. It is amazing how individuals can feel so strongly about popular ideas they know little about" (Smith, 2018, para. 4). It is only natural to be curious about the world and others' beliefs, but do not be so quick to throw away your morals because of someone else's flashy new idea.

Peer pressure and influence are especially hard for you as a teen because you are figuring out your self-worth. More often than not, we value what our friends think of us—ultimately affecting our self-esteem. Amy Eva, Ph.D., says, "When focusing on self-esteem, we tend to get caught up in comparing ourselves. Teens, in particular, often sense an imaginary audience and can become highly sensitized to who they are relative to everyone around them" (2018, para. 14). This is only made more apparent through social media, where you can be obsessive over your number of likes or followers. You might be more inclined to try to befriend those popular in your social circles and find that you might try to mirror them to become more like them. Jacobsen also writes "that peers have a greater influence on adolescent substance abuse than do parents. Peers can encourage friends to use alcohol or tease them for being afraid to try them, which can lead to the initiation of drinking and drug use" (2017, para. 10).

Types of Peer Pressure

Whether you are aware of it or not, your peers can affect many parts of your day-to-day life. Peers "model" certain behaviors to you throughout the day because, after all, you are observing each other throughout the school day. You see how they dress. You see how they talk to one another. "Seeing these behaviors can undeniably pressure you to make the same choices" (Jacobsen, 2017, para. 8).

Sometimes, these socially cued behaviors can be something innocent, like everyone needs to drink out of the same style water bottle; other times, it can be something more at risk to your health, like your friends all starting to smoke cigarettes or marijuana (Jacobsen, 2017, para. 8).

Your friends' attitudes towards sex can also influence you positively and negatively. If your friends are practicing safe sex, it will positively influence your own opinion of being safe as well. However, Jacobsen warns that "having sexually active peers is linked to engagement in risky sexual activities" (2017, para. 11).

Your friends can have a very positive influence on your life. If your friends engage in healthy behaviors, it is much more likely that you will also want to engage in those same behaviors. "Positive peer pressure can help teens develop the coping skills necessary for adulthood. It might encourage teens to become more active in athletics or to avoid risky behaviors, which can be especially helpful during tough times" (Scripps, 2019, para. 5).

Positive influences can take many shapes and forms. It usually involves you making healthy or other kinds of beneficial choices. These positive-pressure peer groups will also help you with your sense of belonging. Here are a few examples of positive pressures:

- "Encouraging a friend to try a new club at school

- Supporting a friend in studying harder and improving their grades

- Peers asking a friend to join a sports team.

- Inviting a friend to volunteer at a charity event."

- Asking a peer if they want to participate in an activity, like attending a party" (Jacobsen, 2017, para. 9).

Negative peer pressure, on the other hand, refers to the pressure to engage in harmful, risky, or rule-breaking behaviors. "Negative peer pressure can lead teens in bad directions. It could lead them to try alcohol or drugs, skip school or engage in other poor behaviors that could put their health at risk" (Scripps, 2019, para. 6).

Negative peer pressure can manifest itself in many ways. It includes, but is not limited to, the following examples:

- "Being asked to try alcohol or smoke cigarettes

- Teasing for not engaging in "cool" behaviors like drinking

- Encouraging a friend to engage in unprotected sex

- Asking a friend to participate in shoplifting from a store

- Convincing a peer to skip school" (Jacobsen, 2017, para. 6).

How to Handle Peer Pressure

Although peer pressure is all around you, there are ways to combat it. Lyness remarks, "It's not always easy to resist negative peer pressure, but when you do, it is easy to feel good about it afterward. And you may even positively influence your peers who feel the same way—often, it just takes one person to speak out or take a different action to change a situation. Your friends may follow if you dare to do something different or refuse to join the group. Consider yourself a leader, and know that you have the potential to make a difference" (2015, para. 36).

There are several strategies you can use to combat negative peer pressure. The most common thought of strategy is just to say no—even if that is easier said than done. It can be difficult because it means going against the group. When you are a teen, your circle of friends can be a very powerful influence on you—so it is important to surround yourself with friends who share common values with you.

Jacobsen suggests that to learn to say no, you must "Plan and practice what you will say if you're pressured to do something you don't want to do" (2017, para. 16). If you practice these kinds of thoughts, you'll be better mentally equipped for uncomfortable situations when they arise—keeping you from getting swept up in the moment. After all, there are many different ways to respond to a situation. Jacobsen says, "For example, before going out with friends, you may practice what you might say if offered a cigarette. You could decline with a simple 'no, thanks' or say that you don't want it to interfere with your soccer training or worsen your allergies" (2017, para. 16). However, it is also completely viable to just say no by leaving a situation.

A big competency of handling peer pressure is being very careful with whom you pick to be your friends. If you have the right group of friends, it will be much easier to have good choices. Jacobsen suggests that "choosing friends who value school and participate in positive activities such as sports can limit your exposure to negative peer pressure. Having friends who support your values can stand up for you if you find yourself in a situation where you need to say no to a difficult situation" (2017, para. 17).

Also, it will help you immensely if you know yourself. While it sounds simple, it is critical to determine your strengths and weaknesses. Jacobsen says, "When faced with the pressure to engage in risky behaviors—such as using drugs or having unprotected sex—it is important to remember your values. For example, maybe earning high grades and acceptance into a prestigious college is important to you. Or perhaps you value setting a good example for younger siblings. Remembering these values will increase your confidence to say no to a choice that doesn't align with what is important to you" (2017, para. 17).

Having support is one of the most important ways to navigate peer pressure. Support can come in a lot of different forms. Your support system can come from a trusting relationship with your parents. Your parents must show you that they are listening to your fears and concerns. When they offer advice, you should do your best to accept it. You can also support your friends—especially if you notice them struggling with any aspect of life. After all, it can mean a lot to somebody. "For example, if people in their social groups or peer groups press them to drink alcohol or do drugs, let them know you are only a phone call away and will come to get them. Teens will respond favorably when they understand that your priority is to keep them safe, not to punish them" (Scripps, 2019, para. 14).

You can also handle peer pressure by monitoring your health. This might mean ensuring you get enough sleep, eat healthy meals, and engage in regular exercise and self-care activities. It's also essential to monitor your mental health by looking for signs of stress. Health is important because it helps give you more strength to hold to your values. Without it, you might find yourself more vulnerable to negative influences.

Having the space to explore your interests while dealing with peer pressure is also important. While it might sound counterintuitive, you need to have the ability to make mistakes so that you can build your own identity.

How to Build Self-Confidence Skills

Self-confidence is the foundation of success and happiness. It is also crucial for handling the effects of peer pressure. A healthy sense of self-confidence will help you pursue your dreams and face your challenges head-on.

One of the best ways to build self-confidence is to work on self-improvement. You can start by identifying the areas where you feel less confident. You can then try to take courses, read books, or listen to podcasts on the subject. It is important to set small goals and celebrate your achievements. As you make progress, your confidence will grow. However, it is important to realize that it's natural to struggle with certain subjects. After all, nobody is perfect. Holding yourself to that impossible standard will only lead to frustration. Remember not to fall into the common mindset that if you struggle to master something, then you must be a complete failure at it. For example, someone with difficulty with math "may decide they're not smart. Or someone who fails to make the soccer team may decide they'll never be good at sports" (Morin, 2021, para. 3). Life is not so black-and-white; thinking so will only hold you back.

Another way to help with self-confidence is to "identify your strengths and weaknesses." Once you know what you are good at and what you struggle with, you can set attainable goals. It will keep you accountable if you plan to achieve those goals (Morin, 2021, para. 5).

When working on your self-confidence, focusing on your efforts rather than the outcome is important. Completing goals and being self-confident is hard work—especially when you are a teen—so praising yourself for working on your determination and dedication is important. If you only focus on the outcome, you may get overwhelmed and quit. Remember, mistakes are learning opportunities, and making them is okay. Instead of beating yourself up, focus on what you've learned and how to improve. Amy Morin, LCSW points out that you can "control your effort, but you can't always control your outcome. It's important to acknowledge your energy and effort so you don't think you are only worthy of praise when you succeed" (2021, para. 7).

For example, it will be better for your self-confidence to praise yourself for all your studying rather than just for getting a good grade on the same exam. In sports, you could focus on how much your practice is paying off rather than just the points you physically score during a game. It's also important for the people around you to focus on your efforts instead of just dwelling on your results—even if they are positive. Morin points out your parents need to show you that it's "important to try hard and it's okay even if you fail all the time" (2021, para. 6).

When you are working on your self-confidence, you need to work on being assertive. While it might sound counterintuitive, assertiveness can be defined as expressing your feelings, thoughts, and beliefs clearly and respectfully. Being assertive lets you set clear boundaries, say no when necessary, and stand up for yourself. Learning assertiveness skills will help you feel more in control, improving your confidence. You need "to know how to speak up for yourself appropriately. When you are assertive, you can ask for help when you don't understand schoolwork rather than allow yourself to fall behind" (Morin, 2021, para. 8).

Morin also states that it is important for you—as a teen—to learn to speak up for yourself because you would be less likely to be treated poorly by your peers. Being assertive means knowing how to speak up for yourself when you don't like how you are treated" (2021, para. 9). You will know you have more assertiveness when you feel confident enough to say no to anything that makes you uncomfortable.

However, it is important to avoid mistaking aggression for assertion. "Assertiveness means standing up for themselves using a strong and confident voice without being rude or yelling at others" (Morin, 2021, para. 10).

Stepping out of your comfort zone and taking on new opportunities takes courage, which helps you feel more confident. You'll soon realize you can achieve great things, and each accomplishment will continue to increase your belief in yourself. You should always try your best to take calculated risks and embrace new experiences.

Morin suggests, "Trying new activities, discovering hidden talents, and challenging themselves can help grow your confidence. But many teens are afraid of failure and don't want to embarrass themselves" (2021, para. 12). Don't let potential embarrassment stunt you. Your teenage years should be spent trying new things, not worrying about taking the plunge. Morin suggests that you can try new things by "joining new clubs, learning to play a musical instrument, volunteering, or even finding a part-time job. Learning and mastering new skills will also help you feel better about yourself" (2021, para. 13). After all, as you belong to "new groups, it will provide you with more friendship opportunities that will help you feel more secure and confident" (Morin, 2021, para. 13).

It will also help your self-confidence if you surround yourself with confident people and observe how they carry themselves. Notice how they speak, their body language, and how they interact with others. Modeling their behavior can help you develop the same self-confidence skills. When others model how to face new situations with courage and confidence, they demonstrate the importance of loving yourself and how it relates to your confidence (Morin, 2021, para. 16). Pay attention to the positive feedback you receive from others and use it to boost your confidence.

Morin suggests that you learned a lot about self-confidence in how your parents conducted themselves. Morin says, "You would have learned the most about confidence based on what your parents did, not what they said. If they were guilty of making critical statements about their own body or abilities, they would have taught you to do the same" (2021, para. 17).

If you have a poor sense of self-worth, it is a significant obstacle to building self-confidence. When you practice self-care by caring for your physical, emotional, and mental well-being, you improve your feelings about yourself. Surround yourself with positive people who lift you and avoid negative influences. Identify your strengths and focus on them rather than your weaknesses.

Morin warns, "If you only feel good when you get a certain amount of likes on social media or fit into a certain size of pants, you'll struggle to maintain confidence when situations don't suit your needs" (2021, para. 16). After all, if you only value yourself on other things, it will cripple your self-worth and, in turn, your self-confidence.

It is natural to struggle with self-worth, as many people do. Courtney Ackerman remarks that could be because "Researchers have a tough time agreeing on what, exactly, self-confidence is. Some say it is simply believing in yourself, while others detail your expectations for and evaluations of yourself and your performance" (2018, para. 5). Ackerman says, "Healthy self-belief is not narcissism, bragging, or boasting. Rather, it is a realistic but optimistic evaluation of yourself and your abilities and a sense of trust and confidence in yourself" (2018, para. 26).

"A student is interested in taking an Advanced Placement class at her high school and talks to her friends about it. Those already taking the class tell her it's hard and she probably wouldn't pass. She could trust in their judgment and pass up the opportunity. Still, instead, she holds firm in her belief about her abilities and signs up anyway" (Ackerman, 2018, para. 30). This student can be you as well if you trust in your abilities.

It will also help with your self-worth if you "practice listening to your thoughts; notice the automatic thoughts that pop into your head and pay attention to the way you talk to yourself. When you notice a negative thought, grab onto it and write it down or just sit and think about it for a moment" (Ackerman, 2017, para. 38). This will help you pinpoint if there is a pattern to your thinking.

Learning to love yourself is important on your journey to developing self-confidence and not falling victim to the adverse effects of peer pressure. After all, "Self-love is not selfish. Self-love is about acknowledging the need to take care of our needs, not our wants, and to work towards self-betterment instead of sacrificing our needs to prioritize the happiness of others" (Asghar, 2022, para. 3). When you love yourself, you are capable of so much more than if you were to be hyper-critical of yourself. It's far more important to have values and true self-worth than focusing on holding yourself to others' opinions on what you should look like or how you should behave.

When you love yourself, you learn to "manage your inner critic to develop a more nuanced view of your failures and appreciate all your effort and personal growth in a kind, loving, and respectful way toward yourself" (Asghar, 2022, para. 10). If you do not know how to love yourself, you can easily get lost in critical thought patterns and become afraid to take risks.

Instead, practice the art of self-reflection. After all, it does not matter if something goes wrong, but when. Doctor Andleeb Asghar says that "Instead of blaming yourself, fail like a scientist to learn from these failures and use them as an opportunity for personal growth. Self-reflection can be a journaling practice, a weekly review, or a meeting with a trusted friend to reflect on your recent experiences and challenges" (2022, para. 15).

When on your self-love journey, setting healthy boundaries for yourself is important. Asghar reminds us, "It can be hard to love yourself when people around you are not respecting your time or acknowledging your value, whether at work or in your daily life. Getting out of the yes autopilot and learning to say no to protect your time and energy is a powerful way to practice self-love" (2022, para. 13). It is easy to get swept up in things and forget to protect yourself. However, you will find that you will feel better about yourself if you learn to speak up for yourself.

You cannot have self-confidence or self-worth if you constantly engage in negative self-talk. Think about your inner monologue. If you think horrible thoughts about being ugly or having no friends, you will truly begin to believe it and manifest it. The more and more you think like that, the more your self-image will tank (Morin, 2021, para. 20). You need to "pay attention to how you internally talk to yourself to learn how to cultivate self-love" (Asghar, 2022, para. 11).

It is important to think about your mental framework when addressing negative self-talk. You must avoid thinking in absolutes such as "I'm going to fail because I'm stupid." It is much more realistic to think that you can instead pass if you try your best to work hard. Being harsh on yourself will only be detrimental (Morin, 2021, para. 21).

Learning to love yourself can be made easier by creating a daily routine. When you "Take time out of your busy day for self-care rituals, whether giving love to your body by exercising or giving love to your mind by meditating" (Asghar, 2022, para. 12). Self-care can mean many different things; you need to figure out the best self-care for you. Some people like to listen to music quietly in their own space. Others enjoy complicated skincare routines. Self-care can also be as simple as taking a walk to think and reflect.

Remember always to "Be compassionate towards yourself. Self-compassion is very similar to compassion toward others (Asghar, 2022, para. 14). While compassion for others is very important, you must extend that same grace to yourself. If you do not, you will only undo any progress you have made toward learning to love yourself. Remember that you are capable. You deserve a happy and healthy life. You are not worthless or unacceptable as you are (Asghar, 2022, para. 1 4).

When building self-confidence, you need to remember that it is a process that requires balance. You need freedom to explore new opportunities, but you also need guidance and support. Find a mentor or someone you trust to offer guidance and advice. Be open to feedback and use it to improve. Building self-confidence is lifelong; you will have good and bad days. Stay positive, keep practicing, and believe in yourself.

Avoid letting the adults in your life micromanage you. Morin points out that if they "Micromanage your choices will only reinforce that you can't be trusted to make good decisions independently. It's important to balance just the right amount of freedom with plenty of guidance" (2021, para. 18). That delicate balance lets you safely explore new things with the ability to succeed and fail. Learning happens when you experience the consequences of your actions.

Chapter 6: Teens and Sex

"Contrary to popular belief, abstinence-only education does not reduce teen pregnancy rates or sexual activity. Comprehensive sex education, including information about contraception and healthy relationships, has been shown to have better outcomes for teen sexual health and decision making" (Stanger-Hall & Hall, 2011, p. 9).

As teenagers navigate the complex world of growing up, one of the most important decisions they will make is how to approach their sexuality. Unfortunately, many teens receive incomplete or inaccurate information about sex, leaving them vulnerable to unhealthy choices that can have lasting consequences. In this chapter, we will explore the topic of teens and sex, focusing on learning responsibility and making healthy choices. We will delve into the importance of comprehensive sex education, which provides teens with accurate information about contraception, healthy relationships, and the consequences of sexual activity.

With the proper knowledge and guidance, teens can learn to approach their sexuality responsibly and make choices that promote their physical, emotional, and relational health.

Being Responsible with Your Sexuality

Sexuality is a part of life, and it is important to be responsible with our sexual choices. Being responsible means making informed decisions about our sexual activities that promote our physical and emotional health, as well as the health and safety of our partners. We can make many different choices about our sexuality, and it is essential to understand the different options available to us.

"Before you become sexually active, you should think about a few things. If you're already sexually active, it's still okay to stop and ask yourself the following questions:

- Why do I want to have sex?

- What types of sexual activity am I interested in?

- What type of safer sex methods will I use?

- What type of contraceptive method will I use?

- How will I communicate all of this to my partner?" (Indiana University of Pennsylvania, n.d., para. 5)

You can make the choice to practice abstinence, which means refraining from sexual activities altogether. You can pick this choice for many reasons, such as personal beliefs, cultural or religious values, or a desire to focus on other aspects of life. Choosing abstinence can be a responsible choice for some individuals, as it eliminates the risk of unintended pregnancy and sexually transmitted infections (STIs). "Remember, abstinence is the only 100 percent effective way to reduce the risk of unplanned pregnancy" (Indiana University of Pennsylvania, n.d., para. 1).

"In short, young adolescents should know that saying no until they are older is important to their health and future. They should know that having sex doesn't prove you are glamorous, attractive, and "with it." Sex doesn't prove anything. Saying no at any age, for any reason, is okay. You might also want to say that kissing, hugging, and holding hands are good ways of expressing affection that adults enjoy. Walking arm-in-arm on the beach or stargazing with someone you care for is lovely at any age. They needn't be a prelude to sexual intercourse." (Steinberg, 2011, para. 20)

Another essential aspect of responsible sexuality is understanding the risks associated with sexual activities and how to prevent those risks. STIs are a common risk of sexual activity, and they can have serious consequences for your health and well-being. It is important to know how to protect yourselves from STIs through regular testing and using protection during sexual activities.

Being responsible for your sexuality also means respecting yourself and your partners. This can include communicating openly and honestly with your partners about your sexual preferences and boundaries and being mindful of your partner's physical and emotional well-being during sexual activities. Consent is an essential part of responsible sexuality, and it is important to obtain clear and enthusiastic consent from your partners before engaging in any sexual activities. "Remember, it's always your choice if you will or will not be sexually active. No one should ever force you or try to persuade you to engage in sexual activity against your will" (Indiana University of Pennsylvania, n.d., para. 6).

How to Have a Conversation with Your Parents about Sex?

Having a conversation with your parents about sex can be uncomfortable and awkward. However, it is a meaningful and necessary conversation to have. Your parents are a valuable source of information regarding sexual health, and having an open and honest conversation with them can help you make informed decisions. They also are a good source of support for you.

According to Laurence Steinberg, Ph.D., "Study after study shows that teenagers want more information about sex than they are getting. When asked how they would choose to learn about sex, nine out of ten say from their parents-yes, their parents-not from their friends, or a health class or books. When asked if they talk to their parents about sex. However, only about one in ten says yes. According to most teenagers, the reason is that their parents hold back" (2011, para. 2).

But why is that? Talking about sex can be a sensitive topic for both parents and teens. "Embarrassment, to some degree, may explain why teenagers are less comfortable than parents talking about anything sex-related, but also, with so much exposure to sexual content in the media, entertainment, and popular culture, teens often feel like they know more than they do. They may think they have a handle on it all when they don't" (Healy, 2012, para. 8). You or your parents may feel uncomfortable, embarrassed, or even ashamed when discussing something as intimate and personal as sex. This discomfort can come from many different influences. In many cultures, sex is still taboo, and discussing it openly is inappropriate. Some parents may also feel like they may not have the necessary knowledge or experience to discuss sex with their children. They may feel unprepared or lack confidence in their ability to answer questions. Parents may worry that their children may perceive them as endorsing or encouraging sexual activity, while teens may worry about being judged or punished by their parents.

Kate Roberts, Ph.D., points out, "Parents must be open and honest about sexuality. Parents need to be authentic and accurate and convey values regarding sexuality. Children should know that, ultimately, they will have to make responsible choices about sexuality. Today's teens report that parents are the biggest influence in their lives regarding decisions about sex" (2014, para. 6). Honesty is essential when discussing sex with your parents. Tell them how you feel about the topic and why you want to talk to them about it. It is okay to express those feelings if you are nervous or uncomfortable.

If you are having trouble talking to your parents about sex, here are a few things you could do.

- Bringing up the topic of sex in everyday conversations can help make the topic feel less taboo. For example, you could ask your parents for their opinion on a sex-related news story or ask if they have any advice on handling your situation.

- Choose a time and place to have the conversation. It might be helpful to have the conversation in a private setting, such as your room or a quiet corner of the house.

When you are talking to your parents about sex, be sure to ask for clarification if your parents say something you do not understand or make you uncomfortable. Ensuring you are on the same page and understand each other's perspectives helps ease the conversation. Conversing with your parents about sex is not a one-time event. It is an ongoing conversation that can help you make informed decisions about your sexual health. With time and practice, you will become more comfortable discussing the topic and asking for the support you need.

Creating a safe and non-judgmental environment can help both parties feel more comfortable discussing sex. Your parents hold a position of authority over you, making it challenging for you to talk openly and honestly about sex. It may make you feel intimidated or hesitant to share your thoughts and feelings.

While discussing sex may be difficult, it is essential to have these conversations to promote healthy attitudes toward sexuality and prevent unintended consequences.

Making Healthy Choices About Sex

Making healthy choices about sex is critical to maintaining overall health and well-being. However, it can be challenging for individuals to navigate their sexual experiences, especially for young people.

Making healthy choices about sex is critical for your physical, emotional, and mental well-being. It helps you maintain good relationships and promote responsible behavior. To make healthy choices, individuals need access to accurate and comprehensive information about sexual health, including the benefits and risks of sexual activity. They also need to understand the importance of consent and how to communicate effectively with their partner(s).

Personal values and beliefs play a significant role in sexual decision-making. It is essential to understand your values and beliefs about sex, relationships, and sexual behavior. It is essential to be emotionally ready before engaging in any sexual activity. Emotional readiness means being comfortable with yourself and your partner(s). Consent is critical when engaging in sexual activity. Both partners must consent freely and voluntarily without coercion, force, or manipulation. Even if you are using contraceptives, safe sex cannot exist if you are not practicing explicit consent. Individuals should be able to communicate openly and honestly with their partner(s) about their desires, boundaries, and expectations. Establishing trust and respect with one's partner(s) is essential before engaging in sexual activity.

Safer sex practices help prevent transmitting sexually transmitted infections (STIs) and unwanted pregnancy. There are many forms of contraceptives readily available to you.

Hormonal contraceptives are one of the most popular methods and are available as pills, patches, injections, vaginal rings, and implants. These methods contain hormones like estrogen and progestin that work to prevent ovulation, thickening cervical mucus to prevent sperm from reaching the egg.

Barrier contraceptives are another type of contraceptive that includes male and female condoms, diaphragms, and cervical caps. These methods work by physically blocking sperm from reaching the egg. They are a good choice for preventing sexually transmitted infections (STIs) and pregnancy.

Intrauterine devices (IUDs) are small, T-shaped devices inserted into the uterus to prevent pregnancy. They can be hormonal or non-hormonal and are one of the most effective forms of birth control. Hormonal IUDs release progestin, which thickens cervical mucus and prevents fertilization. Non-hormonal IUDs release copper, which is toxic to sperm, preventing fertilization.

Sterilization is a permanent form of birth control and includes procedures like tubal ligation (for women) or vasectomy (for men). These methods are a good choice for individuals who are sure they do not want to have children in the future.

Natural family planning involves tracking ovulation and avoiding sexual activity during the fertile period of the menstrual cycle. This method requires a lot of self-control and a willingness to abstain from sex during the fertile period. It can be an effective method for some individuals but may not be the best choice for everyone.

Emergency contraception is a backup method that can be used after unprotected sex to prevent pregnancy. It is available in the form of pills or copper IUD insertion. Emergency contraception is not intended to be used as a regular method of birth control and should only be used in emergencies, but it is available to you should you ever need it.

Chapter 7: Anger Issues

Sarah was always happy and carefree as a child. But as she entered her teenage years, she found herself feeling angry and frustrated much of the time. It started with small things, like getting upset when her little brother wouldn't leave her alone or her parents wouldn't let her go out with friends. But soon, she got angry at school, lashing out at teachers and classmates for no apparent reason.

Sarah didn't understand why she was feeling so angry all the time, and she didn't know how to control it. She tried talking to her friends, but they didn't understand what she was going through. She even tried talking to her parents, who just brushed it off as typical teenage moodiness.

It wasn't until Sarah started seeing a counselor that she began to understand where her anger was coming from. Through therapy, she learned that her anger was a response to her stress and anxiety about school, her social life, and her uncertain future. She also learned how to recognize the signs of her anger and manage it healthily, like taking deep breaths or running.

Today, Sarah is still prone to anger occasionally, but she knows how to recognize and address it before it gets out of control. She's grateful that she got the help she needed to understand her anger and learn how to control it, and she hopes that other teenagers who are struggling with anger can find the same help and support.

Anger is a complex emotion that everyone experiences at some point in their lives. It can naturally respond to frustration, disappointment, or even fear. However, when anger is not expressed healthily, it can become a destructive force that causes harm to oneself and others. Teenagers, in particular, often struggle with anger issues but may not know how to talk about it or seek help.

By understanding and learning to manage their anger, teenagers can improve their relationships, academic performance, and overall quality of life. It is valuable to gain insights from those who have also struggled with their anger.

What Is Anger?

Before you are quick to label yourself with an anger issue, take a moment to remember that anger is a normal emotion everyone experiences. Anger only becomes a true issue when it becomes uncontrollable and affects different aspects of your daily life. Anger issues can manifest in many ways, from passive-aggressive behavior to explosive outbursts. As a teen, you are undergoing significant changes in your life, and you may experience anger more intensely and struggle to cope with those changes.

Anger is a natural response to feeling threatened, frustrated, or powerless. For some people, that emotional response can be mild irritation; for others, they can respond by being sent into an intense fury—as anger is very personal to you. What affects others may not even elicit a second thought from you. However, as Adrienne Santos-Longhurst points out, "Anger becomes a problem only when you have trouble controlling it, causing you to say or do things you regret" (2019, para. 3).

When anger is expressed appropriately, it can be a healthy way to assert yourself or even solve problems. However, when anger becomes destructive, it can cause harm to both yourself and others. If you struggle with your anger, you may find yourself lashing out at your friends, family, or others, causing damage to relationships. If it becomes an even bigger issue, you may get in trouble with the law.

Causes of Teenager Anger

As a teen, you are going through many internal and external changes. Large changes can cause upheaval in your life, potentially triggering volatile emotions. It's important to try and identify things that upset you.

While growing up, you are undergoing significant hormonal changes that can and will affect your mood and behavior. The surge in testosterone in boys can make them more prone to aggression, while the fluctuations in estrogen and progesterone in girls can cause mood swings and irritability.

Your family dynamic can change now that you are no longer a child. The change is a chance to impact how you express and cope with anger significantly. You may also struggle to manage your anger if you grew up in a household where your parents were prone to explosive anger.

Now that you are in high school, you may also find yourself more focused on your academics as you prepare to apply to college. This new pressure can also make you feel overwhelmed and more prone to lashing out in anger. You also will find yourself dealing with your friends as they struggle with different parts of being a teen.

Some other causes of internalized anger can be traumatic events that you could have suffered, such as physical or emotional abuse or neglect. You can even pick up internalized anger if you have witnessed violence instead of experiencing it yourself. If you have any mental health issues—such as, but not limited to, depression or anxiety—you can find yourself more irritable and more prone to unhealthy anger.

Mental Illness and Anger

If you suffer from mental health issues, you may be more prone to suffering from anger outbursts. There are many different mental health illnesses. Mental illness and anger can be a dangerous combination, leading to a potential risk of causing self-harm or harm to others. People who suffer from any mental health illness can have problems regulating their emotions—resulting in intense and unpredictable outbursts of anger.

Penn Medicine suggests that some of the more common mental health issues for teens are the following:

- "Generalized anxiety—Excessive worry about everyday matters

- Social phobias—Severe feelings of self-consciousness and insecurity in social settings

- Depression—Persistent feelings of sadness, anxiety, or emptiness" (2018, para. 11)

These mental health issues all have their own unique set of symptoms to be aware of.

"Symptoms of a generalized anxiety disorder include:

- Feeling restless, wound up, or on edge

- Becoming fatigued easily

- Struggling with concentration

- Experiencing irritability

- Feeling muscle tension

- Having difficulty keeping worry levels under control

- Struggling with sleep, such as difficulties falling asleep or staying asleep, or not feeling well-rested

Social anxiety disorder symptoms include:

- Feeling very anxious at the thought of being around others, and struggling to talk to other people

- Experiencing extreme self-consciousness and fear of humiliation, embarrassment, rejection, or offending people

- Worrying about being judged

- Feeling anxious days or even weeks ahead of a social event

- Avoiding places where other people will be

- Struggling to make and keep friends

- Blushing, sweating, or trembling around others

- Experiencing nausea around other people

And signs of depression include:
- Feeling persistently sad, anxious, or empty

- Experiencing hopelessness or pessimism

- Struggling with irritability

- Feeling guilty, worthless, or helpless

- Losing interest in hobbies or activities that used to be enjoyable

- Struggling with fatigue or lack of energy

- Moving and/or talking more slowly than usual

- Feeling restless

- Struggling with concentration, memory, and/or decision-making

- Experiencing unexplained changes in appetite or weight

- Having thoughts of death or suicide

- Unexplained aches or pains that don't go away when treated" (Penn Medicine, 2018 para. 15-17).

All of these symptoms are very important to be aware of. If you think you feel any of these consistently, it is a good idea to reach out to your parents and doctor. When you catch a problem such as anxiety or depression early, you can develop a plan to live with it healthily. If you ignore these problems, you can make more issues for yourself, which can culminate in misplaced anger.

Emma Freestone warns, "Depression in adolescents has grown increasingly prevalent in recent years and has led Dr. Ali Crandall, public health professor, to study the factors in family life that affect the development of depressive symptoms in adolescents. Using Maslow's hierarchy of needs as a framework for identifying the needs of adolescents, Dr. Crandall determined whether the fulfillment or lack of fulfillment of certain needs in family life was predictive of depressive symptoms" (2021, para. 2).

There, of course, are other mental health issues other than depression or anxiety. These disorders can be very serious as they heavily affect your mood regulation.

If you suffer from any of the bipolar disorders, you may experience intense mood swings, including intense episodes of anger and aggression.

Those who suffer from post-traumatic stress—more commonly known as PTSD—often have extreme social anxiety, fear, and anger, as they deal with the haunting and triggering memories of the traumatic event that caused the disorder. People who have borderline personality disorder may have very intense and unstable emotions, including anger and hostility. People with schizophrenia may experience delusions and hallucinations that can contribute to feelings of anger and aggression when others struggle to understand them.

If you are experiencing anger due to a mental illness, it is essential to seek professional help. Remember that you are not alone if you have a mental illness. A mental health professional can help you develop coping strategies and learn healthy ways to express your emotions. Please do not suffer by yourself. Seeking help can do wonders for you, especially if you are prone to anger or self-hatred.

Recognizing Triggers

Recognizing the triggers that cause anger can help you manage your anger and respond more constructively. It is important to recognize that many things can trigger anger—such as external events, internal thoughts and feelings, or even certain physical sensations. Triggers are very personal, as what upsets one person may not even affect another.

A few common teenage triggers for mood swings and potential emotional dysregulation include:

- "feeling overwhelmed or stressed

- sense of frustration or helplessness

- unresolved conflict or feeling misunderstood

- academic pressure

- hormonal changes

- confusion and low self-esteem

- lack of sleep or poor nutrition" (Himani, 2022, para. 4).

All of these feelings can be common for teenagers. After all, you are in a period of your life where there is a lot of change. You are no longer a child who has things figured out for them. As you approach adulthood and college, you can no longer rely so heavily on the adults in your life to figure things out for you. This added pressure—be it socially or academically—can make you feel overwhelmed. Being chronically overwhelmed can also then lead to intense anger.

If you constantly feel disrespected or belittled by your friends or family, you can have anger manifest through resentment. It is healthy to recognize that your relationships should raise you up and make you feel good, not tear you apart mentally. You can also feel angry if you feel betrayed or let down by someone you trust. Betrayal stings hard and can also lead to your desire to enact revenge—a feeling closely related to anger.

Situations where you feel like you have lost control can also be very triggering. After all, it is natural to feel frustrated to have your day ruined by something you did not anticipate. But that frustration can build into anger if you constantly feel that nothing ever goes your way. That frustration can especially build if you feel that you have a lack of control.

You can also feel more triggered into anger if your physical and mental needs are not met. If you constantly feel hungry, thirsty, or tired, you may be much more irritable and prone to angry outbursts with your friends. If you suffer from chronic pain or general discomfort, you may have a shorter fuse than others. You cannot beat yourself up for those feelings, as dealing with anything that causes you pain is not fun. Do your best to try to address the source of those triggers to manage them.

Recognizing anger triggers is the first step in managing and controlling anger. Once you know what triggers your anger, you can develop coping mechanisms to help you respond more healthily.

Types of Anger

As Santos-Longhurst points out, "Anger can manifest itself in several ways" (2019, para. 38). While a normal and common feeling, anger can take many different forms, as no two people express or even experience anger in the same way.

Anger can take different forms, including outward, inward, and passive anger. Each form manifests differently and requires a unique approach to manage it effectively.

"Anger and aggression can be outward, inward, or passive" (Santos-Longhurst, 2019, para. 38).

"Outward anger involves expressing your anger and aggression in an obvious way, such as shouting, cursing, throwing or breaking things" (Santos-Longhurst, 2019, para. 39). Individuals who express their anger outwardly can be a danger to themselves and others. They also have the potential to be abusive towards others while experiencing an angry outburst.

"Inward anger is directed at yourself. It involves negative self-talk, denying yourself things that make you happy or even basic needs, such as food. Self-harm and isolating yourself from people are other ways anger can be directed inward" (Santos-Longhurst, 2019, para. 40). Inward anger is much more subtle to see in others because it can often be invisible. Individuals with inward anger tend to blame themselves for things out of their control and often experience guilt, shame, and self-loathing. Having inward anger can lead to depression, anxiety, and other mental health issues.

"Passive anger expression involves subtle and indirect ways to express your anger. Examples of this passive-aggressive behavior include giving someone the silent treatment, sulking, being sarcastic, and making snide remarks" (Santos-Longhurst, 2019, para. 41). Passive anger is a less obvious form of anger that often goes unrecognized by both yourself and even others. Passive anger can manifest as sarcasm, silent treatment, or avoiding difficult conversations, which can cause misunderstandings and further conflict in relationships. It can also sometimes suppress anger and avoid confrontation, leading to resentment and a lack of assertiveness in communication.

Identifying Anger Issues

Identifying whether you have anger issues can be complicated, as it requires you to be honest with yourself. Although everyone experiences anger now and then, you have anger issues when it begins to interfere with your daily life and relationships.

One way to identify if you have anger issues is to pay attention to your physical and emotional responses when you become angry. Some physical symptoms of anger may include increased heart rate, sweating, muscle tension, and headaches. Emotionally, you may feel irritable, frustrated, or overwhelmed. You may also experience a desire to yell, lash out, or become physically aggressive in other ways.

Another way to identify if you have anger issues is to consider the frequency and intensity of your angry outbursts. Do you find yourself becoming angry frequently over small or insignificant things? Do you have difficulty controlling your anger once it has been triggered? Do you find that your anger lasts for extended periods and affects your ability to function normally? If you feel like the answer to any of those questions is yes, you might have anger issues.

It is also essential to consider your anger's impact on your relationships. Are your friends and family members hesitant to approach you when angry? Do you have difficulty maintaining close relationships due to your anger? Do you find that your anger affects your work or school performance? If the answer to these is also yes, then your anger is controlling your life, showing that you might have issues.

Santos-Longhurst agrees but suggests that you have anger issues if you experience any of the following:

- "you feel angry often

- you feel that your anger seems out of control

- your anger is impacting your relationships

- your anger is hurting others

- your anger causes you to say or do things you regret

- you're verbally or physically abusive" (2019, para. 42).

If you suspect that you have difficulty managing your anger, it is crucial to seek assistance from a mental health professional who can help you in comprehending the underlying causes of your anger, and provide effective coping strategies to regulate your emotions. It's also important to remember that anger is a natural emotion, and it is acceptable to feel angry sometimes.

Nevertheless, it is crucial to acknowledge when anger becomes problematic and to seek help when necessary. With consistent effort and assistance, individuals who suffer from anger issues can still develop healthy and constructive ways to manage their anger, ultimately improving their relationships and overall well-being and enhancing their quality of life. There is no shame in seeking support for anger problems, and it's never too late to address them.

Managing Your Anger and Living an Anger-Free Life

When anger is expressed in an unhealthy or destructive way, it can negatively affect an individual's mental and physical well-being and relationships with others. If you struggle with anger, seeking help and learning healthy anger management techniques are essential to overcome your anger.

You begin managing your anger by learning what triggers you. As we discussed already, triggers are very personal to you. A key part of anger management is avoiding your triggers or managing them if you cannot fully avoid them.

You can also try deep breathing, meditation, or other relaxation techniques when anger builds up. This can help you calm down and gain perspective before reacting. When we are angry, our breathing becomes rapid and shallow. Taking deep breaths can help slow down our breathing and reduce physical tension during an episode. You can also remove yourself from the situation and go to a quiet place to calm down. A change of scenery, such as going to a different room, stepping outside, or walking around the block, can help regulate your feelings during an intense moment of anger.

You can also practice relaxation techniques such as yoga, meditation, or progressive muscle relaxation. These techniques can help you calm down and reduce stress. Relaxation techniques such as deep breathing, meditation, and yoga can help you manage your anger by calming your mind and body. These techniques can help reduce stress and anxiety, common triggers for anger. "Self-relaxation techniques are a great way to manage anger. You can try various techniques, such as deep breathing, visualization, and muscle relaxation. These techniques can help you calm down and focus on something other than the thing that's making you angry. Finding a technique that works for you and practicing it regularly is important. Moreover, it might be helpful to have a relaxation technique that you can use the moment when you're feeling angry" (Himani, 2022, para. 17). You can learn more about yoga by checking the Yoga Burn program from Market

Shop 73, available on their website at: www.marketshop73.online/y
oga-burn

Mindfulness is being present and focusing on the here and now. Mindfulness is being present in the moment and observing your thoughts and emotions without judgment. Practicing mindfulness can help you gain perspective on the situation and reduce the intensity of your emotions. It can help you manage your anger by reducing stress and anxiety and promoting emotional regulation. You can practice mindfulness through meditation, yoga, or simply taking a few deep breaths and focusing on your surroundings. Mindfulness meditation is the practice of focusing one's attention to mindfully observe and accept the thoughts and feelings that arise within the present moment. According to a recent meta-analysis, mindfulness-based therapies are effective in treating anxiety and depression, leading to significant and long-lasting improvements in emotional well-being (Fredrickson et al., 2017).

Often, anger can stem from feeling powerless or not being heard. Make sure that you are engaging in effective communication. Learning how to communicate your needs effectively and assertively will help you avoid being aggressive or angry about not meeting your needs. Effective communication also plays a vital role in managing conflicts and resolving disputes peacefully. When you express your thoughts and feelings respectfully, you can avoid fighting. You should also avoid using aggressive or accusatory language and use "I" statements to express your feelings. For example, instead of saying, "You always make me angry," say, "I feel frustrated when you don't listen to me."

Miscommunication can also lead to anger, so ask for clarification if you don't understand someone's message before you get angry at something somebody said. Confirming your understanding by asking questions, summarizing the conversation, or repeating various aspects of the conversation can help you if you struggle with anger from constant miscommunication.

Sometimes anger can come from feeling stuck in a difficult situation. Learning problem-solving skills can help you find solutions and take action to change the situation.

When we are angry, our body reacts physically, mentally, and emotionally. Our heart rate and blood pressure increase, and we may feel anxious, tense, or agitated. Our thoughts may become distorted, and we may engage in behaviors that we later regret. Taking time out helps to reduce these physiological, mental, and emotional responses and allows us to calm down and gain perspective.

Taking care of yourself physically, emotionally, and mentally is essential in managing anger. Exercise, healthy eating, and getting enough sleep can help improve your mood and reduce stress. You can also engage in self-care behaviors to help keep your anger in check. Activities that you find relaxing, such as listening to music, taking a warm bath, or reading a book, can help with mood regulations and calm you down when you feel most prone to anger. It can also be helpful to write down your thoughts and feelings, as that can help you process your thoughts. "This means expressing your feelings without resorting to aggression or violence. Finding an outlet for your anger is important, such as talking to a friend or writing in a journal. If you can't healthily express your anger, it will likely come out unhealthy, such as lashing out at people or destroying property" (Himani, 2022, para. 11).

Holding onto anger can be harmful to your mental and physical health. Forgiveness is a powerful tool to help you overcome anger and move forward. Forgiving someone does not mean that you condone their actions or behavior, but you are letting go of the anger and resentment toward them.

Learning to take time out when dealing with anger is essential to manage it effectively. Taking time out when dealing with anger is an essential skill to develop. It helps us to manage our emotions, prevent harmful behaviors, and improve our relationships. By practicing these strategies, we can learn to take control of our anger and express ourselves constructively. Taking time out can also prevent us from acting impulsively, leading to negative consequences, such as physical aggression, property damage, or verbal abuse. It gives us time to reflect on the situation and choose a healthy and constructive way to express our feelings.

Living an anger-free life is possible with work and commitment. You can effectively manage and ultimately eliminate anger by identifying the root cause of your anger, learning relaxation techniques, practicing self care, forgiving others, seeking professional help, communicating effectively, and practicing mindfulness. Remember, anger is a normal emotion, and it is okay to feel angry, but how you respond to that anger matters.

Chapter 8: Money Management

D id you know that nearly 25% of adults have no emergency savings, and almost 40% of Americans would struggle to cover an unexpected $400 expense? If you start learning about money management now, or you may avoid becoming part of these alarming statistics in the future. (Federal Reserve Board's Division of Consumer and Community Affairs, 2022, p.7)

This statement highlights the importance of teaching teenagers about money management because it can have long-term effects on their financial stability as adults. It points out the alarming statistics that show a significant portion of the population is not financially prepared for unexpected expenses or emergencies. By starting to teach teenagers about money management now, they can develop good habits and financial literacy that will help them avoid being part of these statistics and ensure they have a secure financial future.

Money management is a critical skill that teenagers need to learn to prepare themselves for adulthood. As young adults, they will soon face the reality of managing their finances, paying bills, and planning for the future. Learning how to manage money responsibly is important not only for your financial well-being but also for your overall well-being.

Why Money Matters

Money is an essential part of life that affects almost every aspect of our daily activities. It is the medium of exchange for goods and services, making it a crucial resource for survival. Despite its significance, many people need help managing their finances effectively, which can lead to significant problems.

One reason why money matters is that it impacts our ability to provide for our basic needs. We need money to purchase food, clothing, and shelter. Without money, we may struggle to meet these fundamental needs, resulting in health problems, homelessness, and other difficulties.

Christopher Peterson, Ph.D., states that "One of the popular conclusions supposedly stemming from research in positive psychology is that money cannot buy happiness. The problem with this conclusion is that it is wrong" (2009, para. 1). Money allows for you to be happy by giving you access to all the things that can potentially help you achieve happiness. Is it possible to truly be happy without money? Maybe. Is it easier to be happy when you have money? Absolutely. Peterson continues, "Research shows that income has a positive relationship with happiness (life satisfaction), although it is not a straight line. As income increases, its added contribution to life satisfaction becomes smaller. The impact of additional income is greatest among those who have little money, but it does not stop mattering, even after someone is able to meet basic needs" (2009, para. 1).

Money also impacts our ability to access healthcare, education, and other opportunities. People with limited financial resources may be unable to afford necessary medical treatments or education, which could lead to better job opportunities and increased earning potential. "A recent, influential paper argued that the straightforward interpretation of money is that it works like a tool, in that it enables the owner to get what he wants" (Baumeister, 2018, para. 1). Tools have such an understandable meaning. Do you need to put a nail in a board? You use a hammer. You use that tool to get the job done. It has a tangible, direct use that is globally agreed upon. After all, you wouldn't tighten a screw with a mallet. Roy F. Baumeister, Ph.D., argues that money cannot be thought of as a tool because "money depends utterly on what other people think about it. Unless they agree to recognize it as having a particular kind of value that can be exchanged for other things, it is just useless paper and metal. The pragmatic usefulness of money depends completely on a set of assumptions shared by many different people" (2018, para. 2).

When you have money, it provides you with a sense of security and peace of mind. When we have enough money to cover unexpected expenses and emergencies, we are less likely to experience anxiety and stress. When you do not have a lot of money, you can experience fear or, at the very least, uncertainty.

The Role Money Plays in Life

Whether we realize it or not, money plays a significant role in our everyday lives. Understanding the role of money in our lives can help us make better financial decisions and lead happier, healthier lives.

One of the most basic ways money affects our everyday lives is by providing us with the means to meet our basic needs. Without money, it is difficult—if not impossible—to obtain food, clothing, shelter, and other necessities. When you lack access to meeting your needs, it makes life instantly more difficult for you. Financial stress can also lead to anxiety and depression, while a lack of financial resources can limit access to healthcare and other resources needed for physical health. On the other hand, having financial security can lead to a greater sense of well-being and the ability to enjoy life to the fullest—as you do not have to worry about getting the money to cover your essential expenses.

When you have your own money, it provides you with a sense of financial independence. Financial independence is a wonderful, empowering thing. With your own money, you have the ability to buy things you want when you want them. You can buy that new gadget you saw or get new clothes. If you have your own money, you also can go out with your friends and not have to worry.

That's why money has the ability to affect your social status. In today's society, people are quick to make judgments about others based on their appearance and possessions. When you have more money, you have more access to expensive clothing and gadgets, which can make you more popular among your peers. You may also have access to activities and events that require money, such as concerts or sports games.

On the other hand, not having enough money can create stress and anxiety for teenagers. They may worry about not being able to afford basic necessities, such as food or shelter, or feel left out of social activities because they can't afford to participate. This can lead to feelings of isolation and inadequacy, which can impact their mental health.

Money and Happiness

Money and happiness have a complex, misunderstood relationship. After all, "one study cited that a nation's higher-than-average wealth and support for human rights were strong predictors of the well-being of its residents. Researchers at The Economist also reported that 85% of the variance in well-being between nations could be explained by nine factors that included: gross domestic product per person, life expectancy at birth, political stability, and divorce rates" (Pennock, 2016, para. 36). While having more money can provide certain benefits and opportunities, such as financial security and access to resources, it does not necessarily guarantee happiness. Many people with a lot of money still struggle with dissatisfaction and unhappiness.

People often have unrealistic expectations about what money can do for them. They may believe that having more money will solve their problems, but this is rarely true. In reality, money is just one factor that contributes to overall happiness, and it is often overshadowed by other factors such as social connections, purpose and meaning, and personal growth.

Another reason why money does not always lead to happiness is that people tend to adapt to their circumstances over time. Eventually, people become accustomed to their new standard of living, and the initial excitement and joy fade away. This phenomenon is called hedonic adaptation or the hedonic treadmill. "Hedonic adaptation is an adaptation-level phenomenon, which is a term that describes how humans become insensitive to new stimuli, and quickly readjust to an emotional baseline. Therefore, the stimulus needed to create an emotion—like happiness or excitement—needs to be more intense than the last stimulus in order for someone to feel its effects" (Scott,

2022, para. 2). Seph Fontane Pennock agrees by saying "There is an initial spike in happiness or sadness, but as time goes on, the feeling of happiness or sadness caused by an event starts to dissipate, and habituation kicks in. After some time passes, you'll be back at the level of happiness at which you were before" (2016, para. 17).

The concept makes sense. Suppose you find a nice, crisp twenty-dollar bill on the floor. You feel good and go and spend it on something. Perhaps you felt really good about it at the time, and maybe the thing you bought made you feel happy for a few days. But then the novelty of the new item wears off quickly. "Research has found that the first bite of something delicious is experienced as more pleasurable than the third or the tenth. People become accustomed to the pleasure rather quickly, and soon, the same mood-lifting little treat doesn't bring the same influx of joy" (Scott, 2022, para. 9).

"For instance, say you purchase a new stationary bike, which you believe will give you pleasure (hedonic consumption). The bike provides you with enjoyment (hedonic value), but over time, you become accustomed to the bike. One day, you realize it no longer brings you any additional enjoyment at all, and you feel like you did before you even purchased the bike" (Scott, 2022, para. 7). Someone who wins the lottery may initially feel ecstatic and experience a surge in happiness. However, over time, they will likely adapt to their new lifestyle and may even experience a decrease in happiness if they become preoccupied with maintaining their wealth or feel pressure to keep up with their newfound social status.

Despite these limitations, money can still play an important role in happiness. For example, having enough money to meet basic needs such as food, shelter, and healthcare can provide security and stability for overall well-being. Additionally, having disposable income can provide opportunities for experiences and activities that contribute to happiness, such as travel, hobbies, and spending time with loved ones.

The key to maximizing the relationship between money and happiness is to approach it with a balanced and mindful perspective. You need to recognize the limitations of money while also acknowledging its potential benefits. You need to keep in mind your various money goals while also avoiding getting caught up in comparing yourself to others or buying every single thing you desire. You should also try and foster an appreciation for what you have rather than running on the hedonic treadmill.

Money and Relationships

Money also plays an invisible but significant role in our relationships. Financial stress can cause tension and conflicts between family members, friends, and partners. It is essential to have open and honest communication about money to avoid misunderstandings and ensure that everyone is on the same page.

Your relationship with your parents can be tested when dealing with money. Kathleen Mahoney writes, "Good thing for teens, most parents—61% to be precise—are more interested in seeing what their kids are spending their money on than in reading their text messages (2021, para. 2). Mahoney continues pointing out that a "Wells Fargo Clear Access Banking survey showed that teens:

- Want to make purchases using their own money, without restrictions

- Have experienced buyer's remorse for an expensive purchase

- Have paid for something online or via an app that they thought was free

- Have purchased things behind their parents' back" (2021, para. 3).

Your parents also are a major source of how you learn to interact with money. Kate Dore states, "not all parents or guardians are modeling healthy financial relationships for their teens to follow" (2021, para. 11). If your parents have an unhealthy relationship with money, it's more likely that you will develop one as well. Dore states, "More than half of teens have heard caregivers arguing about money over the past month. These spats have included issues like spending too much (45%), bills costing more than expected (37%), needing more funds (34%), and a large expense (32%)" (2021, para 13).

Your parents' relationship with money can also be a source of contention. "One-third of teens reported their parents or guardians spent money on things they didn't need rather than supporting the family" (Dore, 2021, para. 13). She goes on to say, "Kids don't understand why adults make the decisions they do when it comes to money" (Dore, 2021, para. 14). Chang states, "Money problems may be a source of tension and disagreement between family members. For example, children may spend too much money their parents cannot afford. This can place an extra burden on the adults' shoulders. Alternatively, extended relatives might judge a family on their financial standing. Whatever the reason is, having strained relationships with relatives due to money issues is never fun" (2021, para. 4).

Managing your money can also have a significant impact on your other relationships. Money can be used to build and maintain relationships, such as buying gifts for loved ones or contributing to group activities. However, financial struggles can create stress, anxiety, and tension between partners, leading to disputes that can cause long-term damage to the relationship. You need to understand the role of money in a relationship and learn how to manage it effectively. Dore points out that "Nearly one-third of teens are showing signs of unhealthy financial relationships, according to a survey from Junior Achievement and the Allstate Foundation" (2021, para. 1).

Teenage years are hard enough as it is. When you are in a relationship, there are many warning signs to look out for that could indicate that your partner is financially abusing you. "As teenagers navigate matters of love and money, a troubling percentage of young relationships are showing signs of financial abuse. Some 31% of U.S. teens aged 13 to 18 have flagged the signals of financial abuse—which may be controlling a partner's ability to receive, spend or save money—according to a study from Junior Achievement and the Allstate Foundation" (Dore, 2021, para. 1).

You need to be aware of the warning signs of your partner being controlling of your spending. It can be something as seemingly innocent as your friend or boyfriend/girlfriend telling you that you do not need to buy something for yourself. If it happens only once or twice, you might not even give it a second thought. However, if you find that happening a lot, then it is a cause for concern. Dore reports that "both teen girls and boys reported a partner has told them what they could and could not purchase" (2021, para. 3), meaning that everyone can be affected by this.

Dore also states that "most teens, 62%, aren't ready for shared financial responsibilities with a romantic partner or friend" (2021, para. 8). You might feel that responsibility when your partner asks to borrow some money. "More than one-third of teens felt pressure to say "yes" when a partner asked them for money, with boys feeling more compelled (41%) than girls (34%). There was also more of a push among Asian (40%), Hispanic (44%) and Black (45%) teens" (Dore, 2021, para. 4).

One of the most significant issues that couples face is the difference in their financial expectations and goals. For instance, one partner may want to save for a down payment on a house, while the other may want to spend more on travel and entertainment. These conflicting desires can lead to misunderstandings and disagreements, damaging the relationship.

Another common source of conflict is the disparity in financial resources between partners. If one partner earns significantly more than the other, this can lead to feelings of resentment, insecurity, and inequality. It is crucial to have open and honest communication about financial matters to avoid misunderstandings and build trust.

Moreover, another issue that can arise is financial dishonesty. It can be challenging to admit to a partner that you have made a financial mistake or are struggling financially. However, keeping these issues hidden can lead to mistrust and resentment. It is vital to communicate openly and honestly about any financial concerns.

One of the best ways to avoid money issues in relationships is to establish shared goals and priorities. Discussing long-term plans and setting financial goals together can create a sense of unity and help partners work towards a shared future. Establishing and sticking to a budget is essential to avoid overspending. By being transparent about finances and working together towards common goals, couples can build trust, avoid conflicts, and ensure long-term financial stability.

Being Responsible With Money

Money is an essential part of our daily life, and being responsible with money is crucial to maintain a healthy financial status. Being responsible with money means understanding the value of money and how to manage it effectively. By being responsible with money, you can avoid financial stress and live a more comfortable life.

As a "Teen, you have three major sources of income: family allowances, earnings from part-time employment, and gifts and other funds received from parents and relatives" (Alhabeeb, 1996, p. 124). By giving teenagers a set amount of money each week or month, parents can help them learn how to manage their finances effectively. This can include setting savings goals, creating a budget, and understanding the value of money. These skills will serve them well as they grow older and become more independent.

It's important to realize that when you get income that taxes will be taken from them. "Most teenagers are in shock when they get their first paycheck and realize how much has been withheld for taxes. Let's use Mia as an example. Over the summer, she is working 20 hours a week at the local grocery store. Her excellent pay is $15 an hour. Her weekly pay is $300, which goes down to $271.18 after federal taxes. State taxes might lower that some more. She is not going to be very happy about having the government take some of this money" (Mepham, 2021 para. 5-6). And it's true. It is shocking to realize that you aren't coming home with the full salary that you thought you would be. "Teenagers tend to have very strong opinions, and they will not hold back, especially if they think something is unfair. One way to address this issue is to explain to them how the tax system works and then show them how they can take advantage of the current rules: They have earned income, and most likely, they will be under the tax threshold, and their money can start growing tax-free. Nothing like motivating a teenager to beat the system" (Mepham, 2021, para. 6).

Understanding the role of money in our lives can help us make better financial decisions and reduce the negative impact of financial stress. By taking control of our finances and making smart choices, we can lead happier, healthier lives. You can start taking control of your financial future by learning and developing valuable life skills like responsibility, accountability, and budgeting. Creating a budget is a crucial aspect of managing finances effectively. With a budget, you can monitor your income and expenses, prioritize spending, and make informed financial decisions. Various budgeting tools, such as spreadsheets or mobile apps, can help you create and track your budget. "You should look at your banking statements each month to see where you might be able to cut out unnecessary spending. For instance, do you order takeout more often than you realize, or spend more on online games than you'll admit" (Mydoh, 2022, para. 23)? These questions are a good start to help you track your money spending habits, which will then enable you to identify areas where you may be overspending.

To avoid impulse buying, you should consider whether a purchase is necessary or affordable. Impulse buying, which refers to purchasing items without proper planning or consideration, can quickly drain your finances. While it might be tempting to buy new things, it's important to really think if you are going to use that item or not. To help save money, you can track your spending using a spending tracker app and identify areas where you can cut back.

Planning Ahead

Although it may be hard for a teen, having an emergency fund is very important. An emergency fund is a savings account that you can use to cover unexpected expenses such as car repairs, medical bills, or job loss. Having an emergency fund helps you avoid borrowing money, which can lead to debt and financial stress. According to Mydoh, "Everyone, even teens, should try to have an emergency fund. Even putting aside, a modest amount could help prevent financial problems down the road if you need to cover unexpected costs—tomorrow, next month, or a few years from now. That includes losing a job, replacing a cellphone that was dropped into water, or an expensive root canal at the dentist—these are all expenses that could easily land them into debt one day" (2022, para. 6). Do not worry about putting in large sums of money into your rainy day fun. It is very easy to get started by putting aside even small sums of money and letting it grow in investment-style accounts to grow over time. Any amount saved is better than no amount saved.

Planning for retirement is crucial to ensure a comfortable life after you retire. You might think that it's too early to even think about the word retirement, but that's where you're wrong. "Retirement may be a long way off and feels even longer for someone just starting their working years, but there are a couple of reasons that retirement planning is particularly important for young people" (Davidson, 2012, para. 1). Why is it important to start thinking about retirement? Liz Davidson says, "First, there's the bad news. The reality is that changes in the retirement landscape mean that young people will need to save more than their parents and grandparents did. That's because the other two legs of the retirement planning stool, Social Security and pensions, aren't as reliable as they used to be" (2012, para. 2).

You can start planning for retirement by contributing to a retirement savings account such as an IRA or 401(k). It is essential to start saving for retirement as early as possible to maximize compounding interest and your savings. Financial experts suggest that although it may seem unusual to establish a retirement fund for a high school student, teenagers can make significant progress towards long-term savings by setting aside some of their earnings in a Roth individual retirement account. (Carrns, 2018). "A Roth IRA account is one of the best tools for teaching teenagers the power of compound interest. To be at its most efficient, the money should be left in the account for a long time. Since the Roth IRA is a retirement account, it is designed to have the money stay in the account for years. Hence, it's one of the most practical tools for teaching them how this works and, more crucial, how it can work to their advantage" (Mepham, 2021, para. 9).

"First, there's the magic of compound interest that we're always hearing about. Let's take two individuals, both aged 26. One invests $960 a year until age 36 and then never invests a dime again. The second waits until age 36 and then invests $960 a year for the next 30 years. If both earn the same 8% average annualized rate of return, who will have more money at age 66? Even though the second individual saved three times as much as the first, it turns out that the first individual would end up with about 40% more money... In short, the younger you are, the longer your money can compound for you" (Davidson, 2012, para. 8).

"Or parents may "match" their teenager's contributions, putting in, say, $2 for every $1 the teenager deposits, an approach favored by some financial experts. So, if your child contributes $100, you contribute $200. Even small amounts can grow to substantial sums because of a young earner's long retirement horizon. "The longer you wait, the more you will have to save," said Carrie Schwab-Pomerantz, chairwoman of the Charles Schwab Foundation and a financial literacy advocate" (Carrns, 2018).

"Most teenagers are not likely to have $5,500 in annual earnings, but it still pays to start early. Fidelity calculated that someone contributing the maximum amount annually at age 15 would have more than $2.4 million at age 65, assuming an annual return rate of 7 percent. If that person waited to begin saving until age 25, the total at age 65 would be about $1.2 million" (Carrns, 2018).

"Balances in retirement plans like Roth I.R.A.s are not reported as assets on the Free Application for Federal Student Aid, the most common financial aid application, " said Mark Kantrowitz, a financial-aid expert. But money taken out of a Roth account must be reported as income on the FAFSA, which could potentially reduce eligibility for need-based financial aid by up to half of the amount withdrawn, he said. Some private schools use a different financial aid form that asks questions about retirement plans and can consider retirement plans as an asset if they choose" (Carrns, 2018).

"Teenagers can benefit from tax-free growth of investments in a Roth account years before they have the opportunity to contribute to a workplace retirement plan, "Ms. Seaman said. And five decades of growth allows plenty of time to ride out market swings. The earlier you start, the more the time value of money works for you" (Carrns, 2018).

"It is important for parents to emphasize good financial habits while the account is under their control, to help create a 'mental barrier' against young adults tapping into retirement accounts early" (Carrns, 2018).

Understanding Debt

Debt is a scary word, especially if you are unaware that there are many forms of debt. "Good debt is low-interest debt that helps you increase your wealth or income over time. An example of good debt is student loans. Student loans are considered good debt because you are investing in your education and working towards a credential or degree that should lead to you earning more lifetime earnings than someone who does not pursue a credential or degree, which can justify the need to borrow the money" (GetSchooled, 2022, para. 5). "Bad debt is any debt that holds you back from reaching the financial success you want. While credit cards can be helpful in building and establishing good credit, they are often considered a bad form of debt. This is because: Many of them have high-interest rates, around 25-30%. Some companies might encourage you to only pay the minimum statement balance instead of paying in full every month, which will draw out your debt even longer. Some companies will offer rewards or incentives to spend money on your card. This can lead you to spend money that you might not have. If you have a high-interest credit card and pay off your balance each month, then having a credit card shouldn't be a problem. But if you have a high-interest credit card and you are only paying the minimum balance every month instead of paying off your card, the debt will build up quickly, and it will be much harder, and more expensive, to pay off your debt" (GetSchooled, 2022, para. 6).

It's very natural, and unavailable to avoid debt of any form. "You incur debt when you borrow money that you promise to pay back, and this is an essential topic that teenagers need to comprehend. When they are younger and see parents consistently using plastic cards to purchase items, teenagers may not understand that this is money that sometimes needs to be paid back" (DeMarco, 2021, para. 11).

One of the biggest sources of debt is credit card debt. "According to Experian data from the fourth quarter of 2018, just over 60% of 18-year-olds have at least one credit card with an average balance of $3,914.10" (DeMarco, 2021, para. 14). It is mind-boggling to think about owing that amount of money when you are only earning a merger salary. It is paramount that you learn how to responsibly use your credit card from a trusted parent or guardian. Credit cards are not inherently bad, but they can be detrimental to your financial security if you are careless while using them.

But it is important to remember that "having debt isn't necessarily a bad thing. Plenty of consumers take on mortgage and student loan debt in order to make important progress in their personal, professional, and financial lives" (DeMarco, 2021, para. 24). You just need to understand how to use good debt to your advantage and avoid accumulating too much bad debt, because "no matter what kind of debt you will have as an adult - either good or bad - debt is still debt. It's important to learn how to manage debt now to create a solid financial foundation for yourself in the future. Letting debt build up without having a strategy to pay it off can have significant negative effects on your finances and credit in the future" (GetSchooled, 2022, para. 2). "Debt among 18-24-year-olds has risen 104 percent since 1992, and this age group spends almost 30 percent of its income on debt payments, according to a recent study by Demos, titled Generation Broke. The study also points out that credit card companies are aggressively marketing college students with offers of free pizza, T-shirts, or other incentives, and that students are clearly lured by this technique" (Gensheimer, 2005, para. 1).

As a teenager approaching adulthood, one major source of debt that you may encounter is student loans. These loans are designed to provide financial aid for students to pay for their education and are offered by the government, private lenders, or financial institutions. They must be repaid with interest and can be used to cover tuition, fees, books, and other educational expenses.

The terms and conditions of student loans can differ depending on the type and lender. Federal loans, which are the most common type of student loan, offer affordable interest rates and flexible repayment options. Subsidized federal loans are awarded based on financial need, and the government pays the interest while the student is in school, whereas unsubsidized federal loans begin accruing interest immediately but don't require payments until after graduation or dropping below half-time enrollment.

Private loans are an option for students who have exhausted other sources of financial aid, but they often have higher interest rates and less flexible repayment options than federal loans. State loans are offered by individual states and may have varying eligibility requirements, interest rates, and repayment options.

It's important for you to consider your options carefully and understand the amount borrowed, interest rates, and repayment options before taking out a loan. Failure to make payments can result in negative consequences such as damaged credit scores, wage garnishment, or legal action. However, there are options available for struggling students, such as deferment, forbearance, or income-driven repayment plans. DeMarco points out, "Once your grace period—the time between when you graduate or leave school, and your loan payments begin— comes to an end, it can take many years to pay off student loans. Each month, you will have to pay a certain amount to the federal government or a private lender, depending on the type of loan and payment plan you choose. If you understand the toll student loan debt can take on your personal and financial life, you may choose an alternative (or additional) payment method for college, such as academic scholarships or grant opportunities" (2021, para. 21).

After all, understanding all the aspects of your financial life can be very difficult. There are so many ways to earn debt that you might be totally unaware that you are starting to spend beyond your means. Jacqui Germain points out, "Though student loan debt and its possible cancellation dominates much of the national conversation, data shows that credit card debt is also a major financial hurdle for many young people, made worse by the pandemic-driven economic tailspin" (2021, para. 2).

But this fate can be avoided for you if you learn good money habits early. Sometimes, as Genesheimer points out, you have to learn certain things the hard way by personal experience. But there is hope for you to develop better spending and saving habits before you become an adult.

Understanding Credit

Money and credit are two of the most critical concepts in personal finance. Money is the currency we use to buy goods and services, while credit is the ability to borrow or make purchases on credit. Understanding the relationship between money and credit is critical to managing your finances.

Credit allows us to purchase goods or services even when we don't have cash. Credit cards, loans, and lines of credit are all forms of credit. While credit can help make large purchases or manage unexpected expenses, it can also be dangerous if not used responsibly. High-interest rates and fees can quickly accumulate, leading to a cycle of debt. Christine DiGangi states, "Your credit score and credit history have a huge impact on your life. You might already know that credit scores impact your ability to get a loan and how much it will cost you" (2019, para. 1).

You also need to be careful to spend within your means. If you have a large line of credit, you may be tempted to spend that amount frequently. It is wise to only spend what you know you can afford to pay off in full. Making payments on time and paying off balances in full can help maintain a good credit score and avoid late fees and penalties. If you are only paying off the monthly minimum payment, the credit card company will start charging you interest on your purchases. As that interest amount grows, so does your debt.

Credit card debt is a very widespread phenomenon. "In 2019 alone, the rate of credit card balances that were in "serious delinquency"—meaning payments were at least 90 days past due—for Americans between 18-29 years old hit an eight-year high, per a report released by the Federal Reserve Bank of New York. That same year, a poll from Morning Consult reported that 65% of millennials and 52% of Generation Z'ers with credit card debt said they experience some or a lot of stress about their debt. In yet another survey, 35% of those polled reported that their debt makes them feel guilty at least every month; roughly 20% report feeling physically ill at least once a month" (Germain, 2021, para. 3). It is important to learn how to use your credit wisely. If you struggle with it, not only will you ruin your health from the stress, but you can also tank your credit rating, which can affect many areas of your life.

Monitoring credit reports to ensure they are accurate, and current is also essential. Managing your credit is a skill that requires discipline and planning. Creating a budget, tracking expenses, and setting financial goals can help build a strong financial foundation.

After all, your "Credit score plays a huge role in your life. They help lenders decide whether you're a good risk. Your score can mean approval or denial of a loan. It can also factor into how much you're charged in interest, making debt more or less expensive for you" (Di-Gangi, 2019, para. 2).

Your credit score can affect many different aspects of your life. DiGangi states that "Landlords, property managers, and rental agencies typically review potential tenants' credit reports. They look for a pattern of missed payments or other negative information on your credit reports that indicate you may not pay your rent" (2019, para. 4). She goes on to say that "your employment, cell phone bill, insurance and your ability to get cable could balance on your credit score" (2019, para. 1).

It's never too early to start working on getting a good credit rating. The best place to start is if your parent or guardian adds you as an authorized user of their own established credit card. If you are added as an authorized user, you can benefit from the positive credit history of that account. However, it's important to note that the primary account holder is responsible for making the payments, so it's crucial to use the card responsibly and pay the balance in full each month.

You can also look out to get a secure credit card. A secured credit card is a type of credit card that requires a security deposit, which serves as the credit limit for the card. This can be a good option for teens who are just starting to build credit, as it allows them to establish a credit history without the risk of overspending.

It's important for you to monitor your credit score regularly to ensure that there are no errors or fraudulent activity. You can get a free credit report from each of the three major credit bureaus once a year at AnnualCreditReport.com. If you find any errors or suspicious activity, you should report it to the credit bureau immediately.

Conclusion

Navigating life as a teenager is undeniably hard. But now that you have more essentials in your life skills tool belt, you should have a slightly easier time navigating life's ups and downs. Your new-found self-confidence or improved self-image should help you as you learn to handle yourself better in potentially difficult situations. Hopefully, you now have the tools to help you identify the root causes of any stress, anxiety, and other negative emotions and address them effectively, promoting good mental health and overall well-being.

Remember that it's very important to take care of your physical health, as it is closely linked to your mental well-being. Life is not always about achieving the next big thing or reaching a specific milestone. It's also about enjoying the present moment and being grateful for what you have. Take time to appreciate the simple pleasures in life, such as spending time with loved ones or enjoying a beautiful sunset. When you are able to go outside your comfort zone, you are able to truly seek adventure and new experiences.

You now can better plan for your financial success, which sets you up for further success as an adult. You can invest your money wisely and try your best to avoid being overwhelmed by potential debt.

Growing up and living life is an ongoing process, and there is always room for improvement. As you continue on your journey, keep seeking out new opportunities to learn and grow. Surround yourself with positive influences and mentors who can guide you and offer support when you need it.

You have all the tools you need to succeed in life, so go out there and make your mark on the world. Best of luck on your journey!

References

Abi-Jaoude, E., Naylor, K. T., & Pignatiello, A. (2020). Smartphones, Social Media Use and Youth Mental Health. *Canadian Medical Association Journal*, *192*(6), E136–E141. https://doi.or g/10.1503/cmaj.190434

Ackerman, C. (2018, July 18). *12 Tips For Building Self-Confidence and Self-Belief (+PDF Worksheets)*. PositivePsychology.com. https:/ /positivepsychology.com/self-confidence-self-belief/

Acosta, E. (2021, July 10). *Life Without Social Media: Is It Better? | Aglow Lifestyle*. Aglowlifestyle.com . https://aglowlifestyle.com/life-without-social-media-is-it-better/#: ~:text=A%20life%20without%20social%20media%20is%20a%20life

Alhabeeb, M. (1996). *©1996, Association for Financial Counseling and Planning Education Teenagers' Money, Discretionary Spending And Saving*. https://takechargetoday.arizona.edu/system/files/Alha beeb.pdf

Almendrala, A. (2016, June 3). *This Explains Why Social Media Is Irresistible To Teen Brains*. Huff-

Post. https://www.huffpost.com/entry/this-could-explain-why-teens-are-so-obsessed-with-social-media_n_574f7084e4b0ed593f134279

Angelastro, L. (2015, November 21). *Social media and the internet distract students from homework*. Eastside. https://eastside-online.org/news/social-media-and-the-internet-distract-students-from-homework/

Asghar, A. (2022, February 14). *The science of self-love: the evidence-based benefits of loving yourself*. Ness Labs. https://nesslabs.com/self-love

AspenRidge Recovery Center. (2022, January 17). *How Do Drugs Affect Your Life? | Effects of Drugs and Alcohol*. AspenRidge. https://www.aspenridgerecoverycenters.com/how-do-drugs-affect-your-life/

Baptist Health. (2020, November 6). *How Social Media Affects Attention Span - Baptist Health*. Www.baptisthealth.com. https://www.baptisthealth.com/blog/family-health/how-social-media-affects-attention-span

Baumeister, R. F. (2018, June 18). *Why Does Money Matter? The Psychological Meaning of Money | Psychology Today*. Www.psychologytoday.com. https://www.psychologytoday.com/us/blog/cultural-animal/200806/why-does-money-matter-the-psychological-meaning-money

Bava, S., & Tapert, S. F. (2010). Adolescent Brain Development and the Risk for Alcohol and Other Drug Problems. *Neuropsychology Review, 20*(4), 398–413. https://doi.org/10.1007/s11065-010-9146-6

Blanco, J. (2021, May 3). *This Powerful "Reverse Selfie" Ad Shows How Social Media Hurts Our Teens' Self-Esteem*. Modern Parenting. https://modernparenting.onemega.com/reverse-selfie-ad/

Boyles, S. (2008, August 14). *Teen Drug Use Linked to "Problem Parents."* WebMD. https://www.webmd.com/parenting/news/20080814/teen-drug-use-linked-to-problem-parents

Brooks, E. (2022, July 14). *5 Red Flags Teens Should Avoid in Relationships | Power to Decide*. Powertodecide.org. https://powert odecide.org/teen-talk/5-red-flags-teens-should-avoid-relationships

Brown, J. (2018, April 28). *5 Tips For Becoming A More Flexible (And Much Happier) Parent*. Fatherly. https://www.fatherly.com/li fe/how-to-be-more-flexible

Calabia, A. (2001, July 1). *Teens and Sex | Psychology Today*. Www .psychologytoday.com. https://www.psychologytoday.com/us/artic les/200107/teens-and-sex

Carrns, A. (2018, August 24). Retirement Planning in High School? It's Never Too Early, Experts Say (Published 2018). *The New York Times*. https://www.nytimes.com/2018/08/24/your-money/r oth-ira-retirement-teenagers.html

Cascade Heights. (2019, September 20). *Teen Drug Use: Does a Lack of Supervision mean More Drugs?* Royal Life Centers at Cascade Heights | Drug and Alcohol Rehab Center in Washington. https://c ascadeheightsrecovery.com/unsupervised-teens/

Chang, A. (2021, April 15). *Money and Relationships*. Teen Trillionaire. https://www.theteentrillionaire.com/post/money-and-rela tionships

Chantim, A. (2020, January 31). *Addicted to Social Media? Here's the Best Way to Detox*. Good Housekeeping. https://www.goodhou sekeeping.com/life/g30681374/social-media-detox-tips/

CHOC. (2022, April 21). *Why are youths resorting to substance and drug use?* CHOC - Children's Health. https://health.choc.org/why -are-youths-resorting-to-substance-and-drug-use/

Colegrove, V. M., & Havighurst, S. S. (2016). Review of Nonverbal Communication in Parent–Child Relationships: Assessment and Intervention. *Journal of Child and Family Studies, 26*(2), 574–590. https://doi.org/10.1007/s10826-016-0563-x

Crevin, M. (2015, December 1). *The Negative Impacts of Social Media on Face-to-Face Interactions*. Talk Shop. https://www.talkshop.company/blog/the-negative-impacts-of-social-media-on-face-to-face-interactions/

Davidson, L. (2012, July 25). *What Young People Need To Know About Retirement*. Forbes. https://www.forbes.com/sites/financialfinesse/2012/07/25/what-young-people-need-to-know-about-retirement/?sh=7c4169df7977

Decker, A. (2015, June 29). *Is Social Media Distracting Us From Life?* The Odyssey Online; The Odyssey Online. https://www.theodysseyonline.com/social-media-distracting-life

DeMarco, J. (2021, November 19). *How To Talk to Your Teen About Debt*. The Balance. https://www.thebalancemoney.com/how-to-talk-to-your-teen-about-debt-5202023

DiGangi, C. (2019, February 4). *What Is Credit — & Why Is it So Important? - Credit.com*. Credit.com. https://www.credit.com/credit-reports/how-credit-impacts-your-day-to-day-life/

Dodes, L. (2015, March 17). *Spirituality and Addiction*. Psychology Today. https://www.psychologytoday.com/us/blog/the-heart-addiction/201503/spirituality-and-addiction

Dore, K. (2021, September 30). *Nearly one-third of teen relationships show signs of financial abuse, study finds*. CNBC. https://www.cnbc.com/2021/09/30/nearly-one-third-of-teen-relationships-show-signs-of-financial-abuse.html#:~:text=Nearly%20one-third%20of%20teen%20relationships%20show%20signs%20of

Duke , A., & Kerpelman, J. (2021, October 19). *Principles of Parenting: Communicating With Your Teen*. Alabama Cooperative Extension System. https://www.aces.edu/blog/topics/home-family/principles-of-parenting-communicating-with-your-teen/?cn-reloaded=1

Eastman, K. L., Corona, R., & Schuster, M. A. (2006). *Talking Parents, Healthy Teens: A Worksite-based Program for Parents to Promote Adolescent Sexual Health*. https://www.ncbi.nlm.nih.gov/pmc/articles/PMC1784238/pdf/PCD34A126.pdf

Eva, A. (2018, May 21). *Five Ways to Help Teens Feel Good about Themselves*. Greater Good. https://greatergood.berkeley.edu/article/item/five_ways_to_help_teens_feel_good_about_themselves

Evenosky, A. (2016, May 9). *Social Media: The Fake "Reality."* The Odyssey Online. https://www.theodysseyonline.com/social-media-the-fake-reality

Fabris, M. A., Marengo, D., Longobardi, C., & Settanni, M. (2020). Investigating the Links between Fear of Missing Out, Social Media Addiction, and Emotional Symptoms in Adolescence: The Role of Stress Associated with Neglect and Negative Reactions on Social Media. *Addictive Behaviors, 106*(106364), 106364. https://doi.org/10.1016/j.addbeh.2020.106364

familydoctor.org editorial staff. (1998). *Sex: Making the Right Decision - familydoctor.org*. Familydoctor.org. https://familydoctor.org/sex-making-the-right-decision/

Federal Reserve Board's Division of Consumer and Community Affairs. (2022, May). *Report on the Economic Well-Being of U.S. Households in 2021 - May 2022*. Federal Reserve Board's Division of Consumer and Community Affairs; Board of Governors of the Federal Reserve System. https://www.federalreserve.gov/publications/files/2021-report-economic-well-being-us-households-202205.pdf

Ferguson, Kortni (2022) *Maternal Perspectives Toward Parent-Child Communication on Healthy Relationships, Sex, and Dating Violence*. Master's Thesis, University of Pittsburgh. (Unpublished)

Firth, J. (2019). The "online brain": how the Internet may be changing our cognition. *World Psychiatry, 18*(2), 119–129. https://doi.org/10.1002/wps.20617

Fontane Pennock, S. (2016, September 5). *The Hedonic Treadmill - Are We Forever Chasing Rainbows?* PositivePsychology.com. https://positivepsychology.com/hedonic-treadmill/

Foothills at Red Oak Recovery. (2021, March 15). *3 Negative Impacts of Social Media On Teen Boys*. Foothills at Red Oak Recovery. https://www.foothillsatredoak.com/teen-recovery-blog/3-negative-impacts-of-social-media-on-teen-boys/#:~:text=Distraction%3A%20Social%20media%20is%20always%20on%20hand%20on

Fredrickson, B. L., Boulton, A. J., Firestine, A. M., Van Cappellen, P., Algoe, S. B., Brantley, M. M., Kim, S. L., Brantley, J., & Salzberg, S. (2017). Positive Emotion Correlates of Meditation Practice: a Comparison of Mindfulness Meditation and Loving-Kindness Meditation. *Mindfulness, 8*(6), 1623–1633. https://doi.org/10.1007/s12671-017-0735-9

Freestone, E. (2021, April 13). *How Adolescents' Relationships with Their Parents Affect Mental Health*. Public Health. https://ph.byu.edu/how-adolesecents-relationships-with-their-parents-affect-mental-health

Friedman, D. (2021, January 23). *10 Money Management Tips for Teenagers (That Actually Work!)*. Modern Teen. https://modernteen.co/money-management-tips-for-teenagers/#:~:text=10%20Money%20Management%20Tips%20for%20Teenagers%20%28That%20Actually

Fuligni, A. J., & Eccles, J. S. (1993). Perceived parent-child relationships and early adolescents' orientation toward peers. *Developmental Psychology, 29*(4), 622–632. https://doi.org/10.1037/0012-1649.29.4.622

Futris, T., Clarke, M., Call, K., Molter, M., Rylee, L., & Farner, K. (2020). *YOUTH-FOCUSED RELATIONSHIP EDUCATION*. https://secure.caes.uga.edu/extension/publications/files/pdf/B%201537_1.PDF

Gensheimer, J. (2005, June 1). *More teens dealing with debt*. ParentMap. https://www.parentmap.com/article/more-teens-dealing-with-debt

Germain, J. (2021, January 25). *5 Young People on Living With Thousands in Credit Card Debt*. Teen Vogue. https://www.teenvogue.com/story/credit-card-debt-young-people

Getschooled. (2022, July 13). *What Teens Should Know About Good Debt & Bad Debt*. Getschooled.com. https://getschooled.com/article/5785-good-debt-vs-bad-debt/

Gohu, K. (2021, November 3). *Parent and Teen Communication: Keeping the Lines Open With Your Teen*. Modern Parenting. https://modernparenting.onemega.com/parent-and-teen-communication/

Grebelsky-Lichtman, T., & Shenker, E. (2017). Patterns of nonverbal parental communication: A social and situational contexts approach. *Journal of Social and Personal Relationships, 36*(1), 83–108. https://doi.org/10.1177/0265407517719502

Grinspoon, P. J. (2021, January 20). *Social Media Addiction: What is It and How To Stay Safe?* Addiction Resource. https://addictionresource.com/addiction/social-media/#:~:text=Talk%20Therapy%3A%20Talk%20therapy%20works%20by%20identifying%20the

Grossman, J. M., Jenkins, L. J., & Richer, A. M. (2018). Parents' Perspectives on Family Sexuality Communication from Middle School to High School. *International Journal of Environmental Research and Public Health, 15*(1). https://doi.org/10.3390/ijerph15010107

Gupta , S. (2022, January 31). *How to Help Someone With Anger Issues*. Verywell Mind. https://www.verywellmind.com/how-to-help -someone-with-anger-issues-5214482

Hall, J. (2019, September 24). *How to Quit Social Media for a Happier and More Focused Life*. Lifehack. https://www.lifehack.or g/846374/quitting-social-media

Handron, D. (2017, September 26). *How To Adult*. How to Adult. https://howtoadult.com/parents-absence-affect-teens-17368.html

Healy, M. (2012, October 2). *How parents, teens handle talking about sex*. USA TODAY; USATODAY. https://www.usatoday.com /story/news/nation/2012/10/02/parents-teens-sex-talk/1606371/

Himani. (2022, May 31). *Anger Management For Teens | Meaning | Causes | Tips To Manage*. Mantra Care. https://mantracare.org/th erapy/anger/anger-management-for-teens/

Indiana University of Pennsylvania. (n.d.). *Sexual Responsibility*. Indiana University of Pennsylvania. Retrieved April 12, 2023, from h ttps://www.iup.edu/health-wellness/campaigns/sexual-responsibility

IvyPanda. (2020, August 25). *Communication Between Parents and Teenagers*. https://ivypanda.com/essays/communication-between-p arents-and-teenagers/

Jacobsen, J. (2017, June 14). *Peer Pressure Among Teens*. The Re- covery Village; The Recovery Village. https://www.therecoveryvilla ge.com/teen-addiction/teens-peer-pressure/

Jeanne, N. (2012, November 5). *Anger and Mental Illness | HealthyPlace*. Www.healthyplace.com . https://www.healthyplace.com/blogs/recoveringfrommmentalillnes s/2012/11/anger-and-mental-illness

Jones, B. (2022, January 18). Teenage Drug Addiction: A Complete Guide. *Verywellhealth*. https://www.verywellhealth.com/teenage-dr ug-addiction-5213002

Journell, W. (2019). *Unpacking fake news : an educator's guide to navigating the media with students*. Teachers College Press.

Ketcham, K., & Pace, N. A. (2008). *Teens Under the Influence*. Ballantine Books.

Kim, D., Berma, A., Gutierrez, M., & Martin, S. (2021, November 4). *The Effects of Social Media on Attention Span*. The Society for Communications Research. https://curiouscoms.org/2021/11/04/the-effects-of-social-media-on-attention-span/#:~:text=

Kim, J. B. (2021). *Do Relationships Matter? (Duh...But Why?)*. OliveMe Counseling. https://www.olivemecounseling.com/blog/relationships-matter-1

Kliff, S. (2008, May 14). *Teens: Does Being in the Popular Crowd Matter?* Newsweek. https://www.newsweek.com/teens-does-being-popular-crowd-matter-90465

Lieberman, A., & Schroeder, J. (2020). Two social lives: How differences between online and offline interaction influence social outcomes. *Current Opinion in Psychology*, *31*, 16–21. https://doi.org/10.1016/j.copsyc.2019.06.022

Lyness, D. (2015, July). *Peer Pressure (for Teens)*. KidsHealth. https://kidshealth.org/en/teens/peer-pressure.html

Mahoney, K. (2021, December 8). *How teens manage their money — and how parents can guide them*. Wells Fargo Stories. https://stories.wf.com/how-teens-manage-their-money-and-how-parents-can-guide-them

Malik, S. (2018, December 13). *Why Teens Are Addicted to Social Media - PediMom*. PediMom. https://pedimom.com/why-teens-are-addicted-to-social-media/

Marshall, S., Hudson, H., Stigar, L., & Assistant, G. (2020). Perceptions of a School-Based Sexuality Education Curriculum: Findings from Focus Groups with Parents and Teens in a Southern State. *The*

Health Educator, 37(1). https://files.eric.ed.gov/fulltext/EJ1268518
pdf

Mayo Clinic Staff. (2022, February 26). *Teens and Social Media use: What's the impact?* Mayo Clinic; Mayo Foundation for Medical Education and Research. https://www.mayoclinic.org/healthy-lifestyle/tween-and-teen-health/in-depth/teens-and-social-media-use/art-20474437

Mepham, J. (2021, July 14). *6 Reasons Why Your Teen Needs a Roth IRA*. Thestreet. https://www.thestreet.com/retirement-daily/saving-investing-for-retirement/6-reasons-why-your-teen-needs-a-roth-ira

Michaels, R. (2020, December 17). *The Escape Habit: Using Drugs and Alcohol to Avoid Life*. Invisible Illness. https://medium.com/invisible-illness/the-escape-habit-using-drugs-and-alcohol-to-avoid-life-4cc6a902e7fe

Moldes, V. M., L. Biton, C. L., Gonzaga, D. J., & Moneva, J. C. (2019). Students, Peer Pressure and their Academic Performance in School. *International Journal of Scientific and Research Publications (IJSRP), 9*(1), p8541. https://doi.org/10.29322/ijsrp.9.01.2019.p8541

Morin, A. (2021, February 20). *How Parents Can Help Their Teen Build Confidence*. Verywell Family. https://www.verywellfamily.com/essential-strategies-for-raising-a-confident-teen-2611002#:~:text=

Morris, J. (2015, March 8). *Learning to live without drug use*. The Daily Times. https://www.delmarvanow.com/story/opinion/readers/2015/03/08/life-without-drugs/24620527/

Murphy, W. (2022, March 12). *How To Be Responsible With Money And In Life*. Clever Girl Finance. https://www.clevergirlfinance.com/blog/how-to-be-responsible-with-money/#:~:text=How%20to%20be%20responsible%20with%20money%201%201.

Mydoh. (2022, September 21). *Emergency Funds Explained for Teens*. Mydoh. https://www.mydoh.ca/learn/money-101/emergency-funds-explained-for-teens/

National Institute on Drug Abuse. (2007). *The Science of Addiction*. https://nida.nih.gov/sites/default/files/soa.pdf

Office of Population Affairs. (2022). *Healthy Relationships in Adolescence | HHS Office of Population Affairs*. Opa.hhs.gov. https://opa.hhs.gov/adolescent-health/healthy-relationships-adolescence

Paradigm Treatment. (2017, July 14). *Teens with Explosive Anger May Need Mental Health Treatment*. Paradigmtreatment.com. https://paradigmtreatment.com/teens-explosive-anger-need-treatment/#:~:text=Whether%20a%20teen%E2%80%99s%20explosive%20anger%20is%20a%20result

Peel Public Health . (n.d.). *This Booklet For Parents Explains*. Retrieved April 11, 2023, from https://www.peelregion.ca/health/sexuality/pdf/info-parents-talk-teen-sexuality.pdf

Penn Medicine. (2018). *6 Facts Parents Should Know about Mental Illness in Teens – Penn Medicine*. Pennmedicine.org . https://www.pennmedicine.org/updates/blogs/health-and-wellness/2017/may/teens-mental-health

Peterson, C. (2009). *Money and Happiness*. Psychology Today. https://www.psychologytoday.com/us/blog/the-good-life/200806/money-and-happiness

Radwan, M. Farouk. (2006). *why you should never follow the crowd | 2KnowMySelf*. 2knowmyself.com. https://www.2knowmyself.com/why_you_shouldnt_follow_the_crowd

Raypole, C. (2019, December 13). *Healthy Relationships: 32 Signs, Tips, Red Flags, and More*. Healthline. https://www.healthline.com/health/healthy-relationship

Ready Set Life. (n.d.). *How to be Responsible with Money: The Ultimate Guide!* Ready Set Life Financial Coaching - Your Money Coach! Retrieved April 12, 2023, from https://www.readysetlifecoach.com /blog/how-to-be-responsible-with-money-the-ultimate-guide

RehabSpot . (n.d.). *Rehab And Nutrition*. Rehab Spot. Retrieved April 11, 2023, from https://www.rehabspot.com/treatment/rehab -and-nutrition/

Richard. (2019, January 28). *Teenage Relationship Problems*. EnkiRelations. https://www.enkirelations.com/teenage-relationshi p-problems.html

Roberts, K. (2014, July 8). *6 Strategies to Help Parents Communicate About Sex | Psychology Today*. Www.psychologytoday.co m. https://www.psychologytoday.com/us/blog/savvy-parenting/20 1407/6-strategies-help-parents-communicate-about-sex

Rutkowski, C. (2018, July 30). *Early family experience affects later romantic relationships*. National Institutes of Health (NIH). https://www.nih.gov/news-events/nih-research-matters/ear ly-family-experience-affects-later-romantic-relationships

Santally, S. (2018, February 12). *A world without Social Media | Sunday Times*. Sunday Times. https://sundaytimesmauritius.com/ a-world-without-social-media/

Santos-Longhurst, A. (2019, February 4). *Do I Have Anger Issues? How to Identify and Treat an Angry Outlook*. Healthline; Healthline Media. https://www.healthline.com/health/anger-issues#causes

Schad, M. M., Szwedo, D. E., Antonishak, J., Hare, A., & Allen, J. P. (2007). The Broader Context of Relational Aggression in Adolescent Romantic Relationships: Predictions from Peer Pressure and Links to Psychosocial Functioning. *Journal of Youth and Adolescence, 37*(3), 346–358. https://doi.org/10.1007/s10964-007-9226-y

Schuster, M. A., Corona, R., Elliott, M. N., Kanouse, D. E., Eastman, K. L., Zhou, A. J., & Klein, D. J. (2008). Evaluation of Talking Parents, Healthy Teens, a new worksite based parenting programme to promote parent-adolescent communication about sexual health: randomised controlled trial. *BMJ*, *337*(jul10 2), a308–a308. https://doi.org/10.1136/bmj.39609.657581.25

Scott, E. (2019). *How Hedonic Adaptation Robs You of Happiness—and How to Change That*. Verywell Mind. https://www.verywellmind.com/hedonic-adaptation-4156926

scripps. (2019, September 23). *How Peer Pressure Affects Teenagers*. Scripps Health. https://www.scripps.org/news_items/4648-how-does-peer-pressure-affect-a-teen-s-social-development

Siddiqui, S., & Singh, T. (2016). Social Media its Impact with Positive and Negative Aspects. *International Journal of Computer Applications Technology and Research*, *5*(2), 71–75. https://doi.org/10.7753/ijcatr0502.1006

Siebers, T., Beyens, I., Pouwels, J. L., & Valkenburg, P. M. (2021). Social Media and Distraction: An Experience Sampling Study among Adolescents. *Media Psychology*, *25*(3), 1–24. https://doi.org/10.1080/15213269.2021.1959350

Smith, J. (2018, November 20). *The Dangers of Following the Crowd*. https://paretopage.com/2018/11/20/the-dangers-of-following-the-crowd/

Spokeo. (2019, August 15). *5 Reasons a Social Media Fake Life Can't Replace Real Life - Spokeo*. The Compass Blog | Digital Identity and People Search | Spokeo. https://www.spokeo.com/compass/social-media-fake-life/#:~:text=Based%20on%20research%20and%20widespread%20trends%2C%20the%20answer

Stanger-Hall, K. F., & Hall, D. W. (2011). Abstinence-Only Education and Teen Pregnancy Rates: Why We Need Comprehensive Sex Education in the U.S. *PLoS ONE, 6*(10). https://doi.org/10.1371/journal.pone.0024658

Steinberg, L. (2011). *Talking to Your Teen About Sex.* Psychology Today. https://www.psychologytoday.com/us/blog/you-and-your-adolescent/201102/talking-your-teen-about-sex

Subrahmanyam, K., & Greenfield, P. (2008). *Online Communication and Adolescent Relationships.* https://files.eric.ed.gov/fulltext/EJ795861.pdf

Sutton, J. (2021, June 18). *Anger Management for Teens: Helpful Worksheets & Resources.* PositivePsychology.com. https://positivepsychology.com/anger-management-for-teens/

T, B. (2019). *Long-Term Sobriety Usually Requires a Drastic Change in Lifestyle.* Verywell Mind. https://www.verywellmind.com/developing-a-drug-free-lifestyle-to-maintain-abstinence-69444

Tejvan. (n.d.). *10 Powerful Ways to Deal with Anger – Happiness will follow you.* Retrieved April 12, 2023, from https://www.srichinmoybio.co.uk/blog/inner-peace/10-powerful-ways-to-deal-with-anger/#:~:text=10%20Powerful%20Ways%20to%20Deal%20with%20Anger%201

Todd, C. (2023, January 18). *6 Most Common Causes of Anger Issues & How to Deal with them?* Mastering Anger. https://masteringanger.com/blog/causes-of-anger-issues/

Toro, M., & Taylor, T. (n.d.). *The Influence of Parent-Child Attachment on Romantic Relationships.* Retrieved April 11, 2023, from https://scholarworks.boisestate.edu/cgi/viewcontent.cgi?article=1105&context=mcnair_journal#:~:text=

UKEssays. (November 2018). The role money plays in everyday life. Retrieved from https://www.ukessays.com/essays/english-literature/the-role -money-plays-in-everyday-life-english-literature-essay.php?vref=1

University of Akron. (2013, November 13). *Sobriety, spirituality linked for teens in treatment.* ScienceDaily. https://www.sciencedai ly.com/releases/2013/11/131113152605.htm

Vertava Health. (2019, October 3). *Life Without Drugs: Natural Highs.* Vertava Health. https://vertavahealth.com/blog/life-without -drugs-natural-highs/

WebMD Editorial Contributors. (2022, December 12). *Signs of Anger Issues.* WebMD. https://www.webmd.com/mental-health/sig ns-anger-issues

Western, D. (2018, February 21). *How Your Relationship With Your Parents Affects Your Life.* Wealthy Gorilla. https://wealthygorilla.co m/how-relationship-parents-affects-life/

Whitfield, C. (2010). *Healing the Child Within.* Simon and Schus- ter.

Winters, K. C., & Arria, A. (2011). Adolescent Brain Development and Drugs. *The Prevention Researcher, 18*(2), 21–24. https://www. ncbi.nlm.nih.gov/pmc/articles/PMC3399589/

Wisniewski, P., Xu, H., Rosson, M. B., & Carroll, J. M. (2017). Parents Just Don't Understand. *Proceedings of the 2017 ACM Confer- ence on Computer Supported Cooperative Work and Social Computing.* https://doi.org/10.1145/2998181.2998236